FILM AS THE FINAL PRINT OF HISTORY

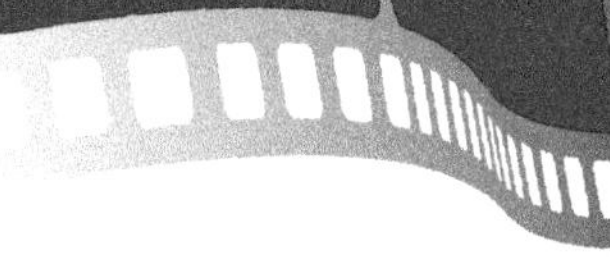

FILM AS THE FINAL PRINT OF HISTORY

The Portrayal of Women in Egyptian Cinema's Glorious Eras

DINA A. MAHMOUD

DR. SWAPNA KOSHY

First published in 2019 by Redshank Books

Redshank Books is an imprint of Libri Publishing.

ISBN 978-1-912969-06-7

A CIP catalogue record for this book is available from The British Library

Cover and book design by Naré Shahmouradyan

Libri Publishing
Brunel House
Volunteer Way
Faringdon
Oxfordshire
SN7 7YR

Tel: +44 (0)845 873 3837

www.libripublishing.co.uk

Acknowledgement

Writing a book is harder than I imagined and more rewarding than I could have ever thought.

To start, I would like to thank my family who are the backbone of my success. Since I was a little girl, I was always surrounded by a family that passionately encouraged and believed in me. I am tremendously proud to be a part of this family and I am profoundly grateful for the courage, support and sacrifices that they have given me.

I was inspired to write this book because of my grandmothers, Fawkia Dessouki and Nadia Abdel Aziz, who have been great examples of strength and compassion.

To my husband who has been by side throughout the entirety of this journey – thank you for putting up with the sleepless nights and the cranky mornings. There have been a lot of ups and downs and through it all, you have been the light at the end of the tunnel.

I am forever indebted to Dr. Swapna Koshy. When I first met Dr. Koshy, I was instantly amazed by her deep knowledge and intellect. She has the ability to not only be a good teacher but to also bring out the very best in her students; even reaching out to them long after they have graduated, to offer her undying support and to cheer on their success. Dr. Swapna took a chance on me and, for some reason that I will never understand, she fiercely believed in me. She stood by me during difficult times and continued to encourage and push me past my limits. She is truly extraordinary. I am incredibly thankful for the lessons and even more for the friendship.

Finally, to all of our relatives and friends who in one way or another shared their support, thank you.

Dina A. Mahmoud

Dedication

This book is dedicated to two strong women who shaped my life – my paternal grandmother Dr. Annamma Daniel who trained to be a physician in an age when women were rarely educated and used her skills to break gender and class segregations.

And, my precious mother Leela Daniel who used her creativity and compassion to bring joy and hope to many and influenced all with her integrity and strength of character.

Dr Swapna Koshy

Contents

Foreword

Being a child in the Mediterranean Middle East opened my eyes to the enormous strength that women around me possessed! At a very young age, I was an avid supporter of women's rights, even though my family was matriarchy-inclined. My father was very passionate about his work as an engineer, which took most of his time, and so we knew that mother was the one who runs things at home. I have always seen my mother as a powerful role model. She was very honest, strict yet gentle and she was very well educated. I loved talking to her, and, I remember being mesmerized by her wisdom. Everybody in the family sought her advice and valued her opinion. She was a woman of high intelligence, perseverance and eloquence. She spoke several languages, which widened her circle of friends to include people from different parts of the world. Both my mother and father were cosmopolitan, having traveled to many countries and made friendships with people from different backgrounds. This made them view things in a more inclusive way than 'traditional norms' would allow. This life style reflected on us while growing up. We were exposed to different cultures yet proud of our roots.

Having open conversations with my parents was a norm in our household, yet contrary to the experience of many of my friends; my father was the one I ran to when I needed to pour my heart out! He is my mentor and he always understood me. He has also a wonderful sense of humour that can embellish any situation with a positive aura. He has always encouraged us to follow our dreams, pushing us to believe in ourselves irrespective of gender. Something he learnt from his dad. I consider my grandfather Eissa, and my dad the first male feminists I knew. My dad used to answer my endless questions about gender equality with a smile on his face, being proud of his little girl and yet surprised how a young girl of six or seven years of age can think of these issues. One of the reasons that made me think of gender inequality at the time was actually TV and cinema, specifically Egyptian TV series and films that are very popular in the Middle East. It was the eighties, and there were a lot of films that gave women characters one of these two roles to play: the role of the ever-sacrificing mother or the role of a prostitute. There were no in-betweens in those films. Although I am inclined to like 'good characters' in general, 'bad' women caught my attention more in those films, because they were rebellious, they voiced their opinions and they were free from society's limitations. It used to bother me though, that women were portrayed in this polarised way. They did not resemble any woman I knew. The 'good' ones were sacrificing their rights and identity for others' sake, and the 'bad' ones were extreme. I did not see women like my mom, my aunt, or my grandmother, who were strong yet balanced. I did not see a woman like my aunt Joumana the poet, or my mom's aunt Anisa, who was a politician and a leader in the women's movement in the United Arab Republic (Syria and Egypt during the union years in 1958–1961). Where did these women go? Why couldn't I see them on screen? Questions like these were persistent in my head; until I watched movies that were produced earlier; like *I Want a Solution*, where the leading character played by the renowned Faten Hamama challenged the system. The film itself encouraged social discourse that led to a change in the law and awarded women the right to divorce their husbands. That is the kind of movie I like and those are the female characters I admire.

My admiration of cinema led me to decide to be a film-maker by the age of fourteen. After finishing two B.A. degrees majoring in Communications and Film Studies, I started working in TV and film and have continued to do so for the last eighteen years, ending up producing and directing hundreds of TV hours and numerous films for major TV stations in the region. I have filmed in more than fifteen countries, which led me to be a juror at the International Emmy Awards in 2018. The most exciting part of my job is meeting astounding people around the world and especially women who showed me many facets of strength. Their strength was lustrous like precious stones and I made it a point to highlight their stories in my films and TV programmes. Women who traveled the world to protest wars and promote peace like Kathy Kelly; women who reached so far as a U.S. presidential candidate like Cynthia McKinney; women who fought their fears like Dr. Fatima Nsour, a twenty-year-old peace ambassador in Jordan who suffered fire injuries but relentlessly carried on her social and charitable work – these women ought to be celebrated.

During my high school years our English teacher asked the class to write an article about what we would like to study in college and why. When I told her I would like to be a film director, she expressed her concerns and highlighted that it was not easy for a woman to follow this path. Her words made me more persistent to follow my dreams. When I met Dina, the co-author of this book, I was reminded of my struggles. Dina is a journalist with a Master of Media and Communications degree. She shares the same passion for cinema that I have, even though our relationship to film was different. In her case, cinema was a way to connect to her roots. As she grew up as an expat kid, her parents used film to bring her closer to Egyptian culture, showing her not only 'modern cinema' but also the cinema of the Golden Age between the 1940s and 1960s. Dina and I also share the view of Middle Eastern women as strong and opinionated. Dina told me that she learnt from the female role models in her life, particularly her mother and grandmothers how to be a leader and how to work hard to achieve her dreams. Actually one of her grandmothers defied all odds and became a diplomat working for the Arab League.

This background has led her to focus her research on film and women in film, particularly in Egypt, an area that still needs a lot of academic research, as it is rich with examples and differing narratives and points of view. She teamed up with Associate Professor Dr. Swapna Koshy who is an award-winning teacher and researcher specialising in communication research covering media, marketing and business communication. Dr. Koshy has received a Vice Chancellor's citation for Outstanding Contribution to Teaching and Learning and awards for Teaching and Research Excellence, Assessment Design and Leadership. Her industry experience includes stints with film, television and radio and this experience along with her interest in the sociological study of films drew her to Dina's research.

There is an interest in Arab culture globally; however, most information in the public domain is tainted and pictures Arabs as regressive. This book will challenge stereotypes and the one-sided portrayal of Arabs and their culture. It will generate interest among film enthusiasts and scholars studying topics in the humanities and social sciences. Film as the Final Print of History: The Portrayal of Women in Egyptian Cinema's Glorious Eras is a much needed book in these times of global change, discussing the portrayal of women in Egyptian cinema in the Golden Age and recent years. Through a meticulous analysis of twenty Egyptian films and their reflection of reality, questions like these are raised: Are the female characters victors or victims of the patriarchal system? Do they represent the women of Egypt? Do they contribute to social life? In this book, Dina and Dr. Koshy show how film not only reflects reality but shapes it too. This book is distinctive as it attempts a content analysis of films from two eras using social realities as a touchstone to assess how well they mirror life. The rise and fall in the fortunes of women are reflected in the films produced too. Film, thus, becomes the final draft of history!

Abir Alsayed

Film-maker and Producer

Introduction

If journalism is the first draft of history, film can be considered the final print. Films can immortalize events by making a historical record for posterity. Art may be for art's sake but film is more than art, conversing with audiences in a tactile manner as no other art form can; mesmerizing the senses and transporting audiences to eras and locales far removed from them. Like creators of other arts, film-makers are influenced by the sociological and political milieu they work in. Therefore, films too reflect the socio-political realm they are birthed in adding to their value as a source of information on various epochs.

Film as an industry has played its part in shaping the cultural and economic world. The colossal industries of Hollywood and Bollywood are recognized globally as industry leaders in the West and South Asia respectively. In the Arab world, the Egyptian film industry, dominated for over a century exporting films and along with it its language and culture to the pan-Arab world. The richness of its culture, coupled with prolonged periods of economic and political stability and prosperity and a liberal world view made the Egyptian ethos a fertile ground for the film industry. The more conventional Arab societies which were closed to most arts, including film, readily accepted Egyptian film productions and enjoyed the fare. Lebanon, made a mark as the film capital of the Arab world for a season but it was short lived due to political instability in the country. Though Kuwait had a theatrical culture, unlike its other GCC counterparts, it did not generate a robust film industry. Today, all members of the Gulf Co-operative Council host film festivals regularly. In the last decade, the UAE with its many film festivals and incentives to film-makers has been recognized internationally as a major player in the global film industry. Both local and foreign films produced in the country have garnered international attention. The late bloomer, the Kingdom of Saudi Arabia, which was a major patron of Egyptian film, surprised the world in 2018 by opening numerous cinemas for the public. The Kingdom has seen the mushrooming of film schools and its most celebrated film maker Haifaa al-Mansour is a woman.

In this changing scenario, where Egyptian cinema no more monopolizes the pan-Arab film industry it would be interesting to take stock of the growth and influence of Egyptian cinema – past and present. This book attempts to look at two prolific and distinct periods in Egyptian film history to study if societal changes are mirrored on celluloid. To sharpen the focus, the depiction of women is reviewed as societal transformations leave the deepest impact on its female subjects.

Chapter one follows the waxing and waning of Egypt's film industry starting with its inception in the late 1800s, moving to the period of sound and the popularity of musicals in the early 1900s. The Golden Age from 1940–60 which was a period of unprecedented prolificacy was followed by a lean period where the volatile political situation caused reputed film-makers to leave the motherland. The advent of television and how the film industry adapted to stay relevant is also highlighted. The final stage covered is the pre and post Arab Spring era which was marked by socio-political changes that affected the film industry too.

The second chapter traces women's place on the reel and in real life. Their role in the 1919 nationalist movement and the first public rally they participated in for political independence transformed into a clarion call for women's liberation. The 1952 revolt against monarchy too had a similar effect, ending in a new constitution being drafted that awarded women equality in many spheres. In the 2011 revolution also women played an active role both on the streets and online. However, films of the early periods portrayed women as subservient to the patriarchal system and confined to the home with no social role.

Twenty films, ten each from the Golden Age and the pre-post revolution period, are chosen for detailed analysis in Chapters 3 and 4. All films had women playing significant roles. An analysis of the profession, education level, activism, dressing and life style of the women characters generated interesting results. The Golden Age characters were Western in dress and lifestyle often drinking alcohol and breaking social norms. They were also highly educated and mostly career women. The two illiterate sisters featuring in *Raya wa Sakina* were criminal masterminds and leaders of a gang of men! And the story line is based on real events. In the films from fifty years later among the lead women there were more uneducated and unemployed women and expectedly they were more subservient to traditions.

Chapter 5 compares the findings from the analyses of the two sets of films from the Golden Age and pre/post revolution periods. Theoretical models including Habermas' Public and Private sphere and concepts of institutional sexism and nationalism are discussed and the saga of Egyptian women's fight for freedom is chronicled.

This book is a tribute to all women, both still oppressed and liberated, and all brave women who fought many a battle for equality in cloistered homes or public streets. We celebrate women who created and depicted celluloid heroines and used film and media as a platform to herald social change. Most importantly, we also acknowledge the role played by progressive men who have worked for the liberation of women both on and off screen. As equals let us stand together respecting differences and relishing our different roles in society.

We are grateful to film-maker Abir Alsayed, juror of the International Emmy Awards 2018, who has created an appropriate *mise en scène* introducing the book. It is only befitting that an Arab woman film-maker who has made a mark on the international film scene introduces this book. She is among the growing pantheon of Arab stars who have broken the glass ceiling. Over fifty years ago Omar Sharif immortalised *Lawrence of Arabia* turning the spotlight on Egyptian film and winning an academy nomination for best supporting actor. Egyptians continue to play impressive roles in the international film scene. Rami Malek who won the Academy Award for Best Actor in 2019 became the first actor of Egyptian/Arab ancestry to win the coveted prize. In the remake of Aladdin (2019), Egyptian/Canadian, Mena Massoud, plays the eponymous hero sharing the screen with Will Smith. And, the show goes on....

CHAPTER 1

Egyptian Cinema: the Journey So Far

Egypt began its cinematic journey in as early as 1896 (only a few months after the first screening in Europe), when the Lumières' Cinématographe was brought to Cairo and Alexandria. The films were exhibited in backrooms of cafes for the large number of foreign settlers who resided in the two large cities (Salama, 2018; p.10). The target audience comprised entrepreneurs and most of them had links to the Western world. In 1897 the Cinematographe Lumière in Alexandria began offering regular screenings, and it eventually became common in Egypt to present films during theater performances. In 1906 the French company Pathé constructed the first regular cinema on Egyptian soil, in Cairo. Apart from this, two additional Cinématographes were to be run in both Cairo and Alexandria. The first movie theatres in the Arab world were owned by foreigners or by immigrant European minorities. In the same way, film production initially remained confined to foreign and non-native investors (Shafik 2007; p. 10).

The film industry later gained significant support from some of the country's most powerful financial houses, the main one being Bank Misr, which aided Misr Studio's inauguration in 1935. Thus began the rise of Egyptian Cinema and the era of the 'Asr al Zahaby,' also known as the Golden Age of Egyptian cinema, which took place between the 1940s and 1960s (Nowell-Smith 1996; p. 662).

Egyptian cinema continued to boom past the post-war period and production levels rose to more than fifty films per year. The Egyptian film industry made a huge impact on Arab cinema, leading to the Egyptian dialect becoming the most recognized form of Arabic in Middle Eastern films (Nowell-Smith 1996; p. 663). Though musicals were the most produced genre, many serious themes including social commentary emerged in the early 1950s. Works of writers like the legendary Egyptian Nobel laureate, Naguib Mahfouz, held a mirror up to Egyptian society.

The film industry in Egypt suffered a major set-back in the late 1980s and early 1990s, when television soap operas became popular and vied with cinema for audience attention. The cinema industry had to reinvent itself to stay relevant. The genre of political satire was embraced and was well received. In the pre/post Arab Spring era too political satire helped garner audiences for Egyptian films. The effect of these films on the Egyptian psyche helped trigger the age of liberation and films were used to publicly promote concepts of freedom and engage audiences in the fight for justice sparking the 2011 uprising in Egypt (Valassopoulos 2013; p. 176).

The Egyptian film industry has to date produced more than 3,000 films since the mid-1920s by an estimated 400 different directors. The films get recognized across the whole of the Middle East and get the widest releases throughout the region on both television and cinema screens. It has always dominated the big screen throughout the Arab world with its mass production of films, which often matched Hollywood standards. Egyptian cinema however, was not always as prolific as it is today, with political unrest and foreign occupation in the early 1900s, the Egyptian cinema industry went through several challenges.

From silence to sound: 1920s – 1930s

The cinema industry began to blossom during the silent era of the 1920s to 1930s. In 1922, Mohamed Bayoumi produced the first Egyptian short film, titled *Al Bash Kateb* (*The Civil Servant)* (Armes 1987; p. 197). Shortly after, 13 additional films were created from 1926–1932. Artists and film enthusiasts were not the only ones who were interested in cinema. Talaat Harb, a nationalist entrepreneur and founder of the Misr Bank, invested in developing an independent industry in Egypt in the early 1920s (Nowell-Smith 1996; p. 662). In 1925 Harb, believing that cinema was a good investment, developed Sharikat Misr li-l Sinima wa-l- Tamthil (Egypt's Company for Cinema and Performance Arts), which aimed to create marketing and informational films (Shafik 2007; p. 14). In 1934, Harb built Misr Studio, which featured a laboratory and sound studio, and hired a number of European specialists, including German director Fritz Kramp and set designer Robert Schargenberg (Nowell-Smith 1996; p. 662). Harb also invested in young Egyptians, who he sent to study on scholarships to Europe (Shafik 2007; p. 14). The Egyptian government considered cinema a commercially viable industry and a source of tax revenue as tax rates were higher than that in the West (Nowell-Smith 1996; p. 662).

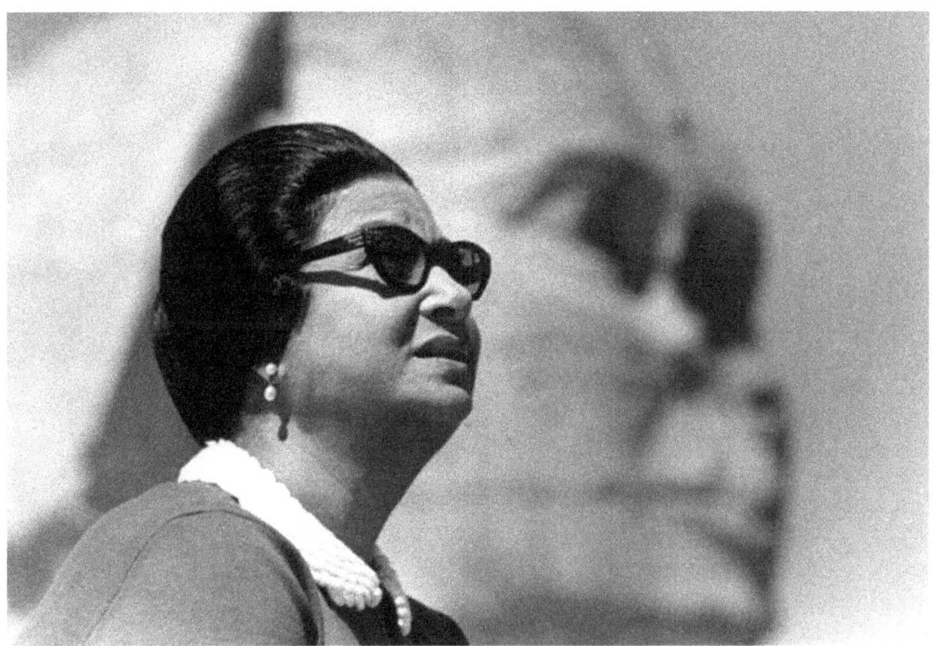

Egyptian singer Umm Kalthoum, known as Kawkab al sharq (Star of the East), is one of the most popular and beloved singers in Arab history.

The era of musicals: 1930s –1940s

The advent of sound in Egyptian cinema, allowed for famous and reputable singers like Muhammad Abd al-Wahab and Umm Kalthoum who were already popular on the radio, to work on musicals. This gave a powerful advantage to the cinema in Egypt, compared to other Arab cinema industries (Nowell-Smith 1996; p. 662). Both men and women starred in such musicals, which made song sequences a prominent feature of Egyptian cinema from the 1930s onwards. Musical films gained rapid popularity from their inception, and the use of acclaimed poetry added to their popularity (Bandhauer and Royer 2015; p. 49).

Egypt's multicultural society made it easier, compared to other countries in the region, to successfully establish a widely recognized film industry. Egypt was home to a number of different nationalities including British,

Greek, Armenian, Italian, French, Syrians and more (Goldschmidt 2013; 40). Films with pertinent messages and musicals appealed to all nationalities (Nowell-Smith 1996; p. 294).

The use of dialect and familiar music and songs helped the audience further connect with the films. Egyptian musicals made their debut in 1932, with Mario Volpi's *Anshudat al Fuad* (*The song of the heart*), which was also Egypt's first sound film (Nowell-Smith 1996; p. 662). Later, adaptations of stage musicals were promoted. Makers of musical films and Egyptian singers such as Mohammed Abdel Wahab, Umm Kalthoum and later Farid Al-Attrache, all gained a massive fan base throughout the Arab world. Egyptian musicals gained more popularity around the 1950s and 1960s, when they introduced scenes with singing and dancing combined, which was unusual as the two arts were not usually combined (Shafik 2007; p. 24). Abdel Halim Hafez, endearingly called the Egyptian nightingale, was one of the first singers to partake in the musicals. He was given a choreographed dance routine combined with his singing scenes (Creekmur and Mokdad 2012; p. 216). Hafez became one of the most popular singers and actors of his time, making a name for himself, as one of the prominent musical stars of Egyptian cinema in the Golden Age.

Aside from traditional Egyptian musicals, genres including melodrama, farce and adventure films were added. Early Egyptian films often comprised comedic circumstances and fairytale stories in the style of the *Arabian Nights* or tragic love stories, all of which were accompanied with music and dance. At the end of World War II, Egyptian musicals underwent a noticeable change. Instead of unrequited love, it became common to make films with an obligatory happy ending. It became the norm for musical films to have at least one dance number, which was often a belly dance. The genre showcased beautiful women, wearing scanty belly dancing attire and performing an intimate dance to a male audience – usually at a bar or a cabaret.

Badia Masabni a well-known dance theater in Egypt, was the training ground for several distinguished belly dancers, who performed in cinema. Some of the dancers borrowed their music list from nightclubs and folklore (Nowell-Smith 1996; p. 32). Aside from belly dance, Egyptian films also tried to reconstruct the dance of the *djawari* (exotic, singing, slave girls), which brought together the elements of ballet and oriental dance participated in by both single and married men. In this period women were perceived as delicate, elegant and seductive, which often led to them being objectified for their beauty (Shafik 2007; p. 103).

The golden age: 1940–1960

As the cinema in Egypt began to dominate the region, many Egyptian producers progressively took control of the film market throughout the Arab world. Though Egyptian cinema's progress began slowly, it soon gained rapid momentum, doubling the number of feature films produced. Misr Studio was the reason for this sudden spurt that allowed the Egyptian film industry to reach its first peak in 1945, when it produced twenty-five films a year (Nowell-Smith 1996; p. 662). Misr Studio focused its efforts on creating and producing feature films and provided opportunities to edit the films shot by shot, within Egypt (Bandhauer and Royer 2015; p. 40). The films produced in Egypt represented the culture and tradition of the country. In 1948, an additional six studios were built and the total number of full-length features produced reached 345. Between 1945 and 1952 Egyptian film production reached an average of forty-eight films per year, a number comparable to today's output (Nowell-Smith 1996; p. 663).

Several prominent directors also emerged from 1945 onwards. Amongst them was Salah Abou Seif, who became one of the more predominant figures in Egyptian cinema. Along with cinematographer Youssef Chahine, he spearheaded the neo-realist movement (Armes 1987; p. 201). Having created dozens of films in the span of two decades, Abou Seif specialized in tightly scripted studio dramas, with a realistic approach to each scenario. Films such as *Raya wa Sakina* (*Raya and Sakina*) 1953, which tells the story of two notorious sisters who were serial killers and the first female duo in modern Egypt to receive the death sentence, were amongst his dramatic, realistic thrillers. From 1963–1965, Abou Seif served as head of the General Organization of Egyptian Cinema and continued to explore other genres such as historical, romance and mystery. The films he directed at the time included *Cairo '30* (1966) and *Al-Qadiya* (1968) (Nowell-Smith 1996; p. 663).

Chahine started his work as an assistant director, but soon became a key figure in Egyptian films in the 1950s by directing a series of films that included social dramas, melodrama and historical epics (Nowell-Smith 1996; p. 664). His films were unique because he used cinematic artistry with mature editing techniques and at a fraction of the regular cost (Khoury 2010; p. 36).

The rise of nationalism and exodus of film-makers: 1960–1980

The advent of colour in Egyptian cinema happened in the mid-1950s and became a regular feature in the 1960s and 1970s. Audiences' interest in sound and colours led to the development of related technology. Additional to this, many Egyptian producers and directors stepped forward to create a nationalist movement in the cinema industry producing films locally. The film industry grew in size as more films were produced in the 1960s by Chahine and Abou Seif. However, the nationalization of the industry proved to be a financial disaster causing a major setback (Nowell-Smith 1996; p. 665). The production of films averaged around fifty per year in the 1960s and many Egyptian film-makers and producers moved abroad for better opportunities, making it difficult for the local film industry to grow (Nowell-Smith 1996; p. 663).

Though the nationalized film industry came to a halt in 1972, the Higher Cinema Institute in Cairo continued to operate, making Egypt the only Arab country to train its own film-makers locally (Nowell-Smith 1996; p. 665). Led by Mohamed Khan in the 1970s and early 1980s, the institute remained faithful to the cinematic history and style of Egyptian film making (Khoury 2010; p. 18). As the film industry advanced in Egypt and around the world, more film schools with new ideas catering to the new generation of film professionals began to emerge.

Television and the new trends in cinema: 1980 to present

The 1980s to the early 2000s saw a rapid decline in the cinema industry, as audiences stopped patronizing cinema turning their attention to television instead (Dwyer 2004; p. 11). Television shows and series created a buzz amongst audiences, who were interested in daily dramas, rather than an occasional two-hour film. Keeping the film industry relevant in Egypt, the 1990s used films to highlight important social issues and historical events that were previously unnoticed and censored. The new films which had themes that were relatable to the audience began to draw viewers back to the cinemas though in small numbers.

After former Egyptian president Anwar Sadat's policy of 'infitah' (opening the door), allowed for private investments in Egypt in 1973, the cinema and television industry began to rapidly revolutionize. In the late 1970s and 1980s television became popular amongst the Egyptian people and cinema became an increasingly commercial enterprise. The large number of television shows and series that were produced in Ramadan helped television to grow ahead of film. Studios that were previously producing some of Egypt's greatest films were used for television productions instead (Leaman 2001; p. 30).

Along with the 'infitah' project the introduction of national television and the spread of the video cassette recorder (VCR) were primary reasons for the shift of audience focus from cinema to television. Public television was monitored by the Egyptian Radio and Television Union (ERTU). Film production declined to ten to fifteen films fewer per year during this decade in comparison to the previous decades of the post Golden Age of cinema. Additionally, the decline in film production caused a number of movie theatres to shut down as the television industry continued to flourish (Leaman 2001; p. 30). This setback was overcome by airing films on national television, which consequently helped to popularize and conserve films of the Golden Age keeping its legacy and value for several succeeding decades and up to this day.

With the introduction of television and VCRs, the habits of Egyptian people, particularly women, drifted from going to the cinema to staying at home and watching programs on television. This pattern was observed throughout the Gulf region, primarily in Saudi Arabia where public theatres were prohibited. In 1984 there was a boom of 'muqawalat' or entrepreneur films which were directed by amateurs and featured unknown and substandard actors. These films were distributed on video and helped keep the film industry alive in Egypt (Ginsberg & Lippard 2010; p. 126).

The early 1990s saw the introduction of 'new realist films'. Well-known film-makers such as Youssef Chahine (who had gained rapid popularity during the 1950s and 1960s) and Bashir el-Dik were involved in this new wave of films. They focused their attention on their own narratives that highlighted the corruption and other evils in the social system. They changed their focus from collaborating with literary giants and their fictional tales to real life social issues and used well-known and credible stars, helping the film industry to thrive yet again. With the help of popular television satellite channels – Rotana and Melody – the film industry, along with theatre and the music industry, popularized the digital video (Ginsberg & Lippard 2010; p. 125). Although the films were well received much more needed to be done to revive the film industry.

As the film industry began to decline, a collaboration among the television satellite channels took shape and they focused on soap operas. This collaboration was deemed to be a success as popular film stars and television personalities like Nour El-Sherif and Yousra were able to work together. The soap operas had a loyal following as they often retold stories of the lives of famous Egyptian legends (including singers and actors from the Golden Age) who contributed largely to the growing cinema industry.

In the late 1990s, production numbers fell to about 20 films annually (Armes 2015; pp. 7–8). However, in the millennial decade, the cinema industry gained popularity once again with a strategic emphasis on taboo social and political issues.

This boom was short lived. After establishing a dominant position in the Arab film world as the 'Hollywood on the Nile' the industry came to a standstill with the uprising in 2011. Countrywide curfews led to the reduction in cinema audiences and as a result film production slowed down dramatically. With the ousting of Mubarak in 2011, and the overthrow of Mohamed Morsi in 2013, the country was left in a state of instability post-revolution. After years of instability it was only in 2016 that the Egyptian film industry finally began to make a major comeback. In 2016, the reception awarded to the romantic comedy *Hepta* proved that cinema is gaining popularity yet again in Egypt. The film broke box office records for the genre by making more than $3 million (Monks 2016).

A number of films focusing on politics in Egypt have been released in recent times. Productions such as *Eshtebak* (*Clash*), which talks about a clash between pro and anti-Muslim Brotherhood demonstrators following the overthrow of former president and Muslim Brotherhood member Mohamed Morsi, received international critical acclaim. The movie received strong reviews at the Cannes Film Festival and was tipped for an Oscar nomination (Monks 2016).

Sherif Mandour, film producer and executive board member of the government's Chamber of Cinema, believes that Egypt's cinema and film industry is recovering powerfully. Mandour claimed that forty films were produced in 2016 and there were plans to release around sixty films in 2017. This is a remarkable growth compared to the twenty films that were produced in 2011. While speaking with CNN, Mandour commented that he believes Egyptian cinema will rise again, 'After the revolution it was not secure to go to cinemas but now people are going again, and it is becoming a fruitful business', (Monks, 2016) . Mandour added that funding for film-makers was increased by the government from 20 million Egyptian Pounds to 50 million Egyptian Pounds annually (Monks 2016).

Mandour admits that although rival Arab film industries such as Morocco and Algeria have stolen the spotlight from Egypt, cinema is a matter of national pride in Egypt. Thus, it is a national priority to regain dominance in the film industry once again. 'Cinema was a huge part of our soft power over history... . It is not the same now and the competition is increasing, but Egypt has a space because we have the only language that is understood in all 22 Arab countries' (Monks 2016).

Director Hala Khalil claims that studios in Egypt have unbridled power and often insist on what she calls 'popcorn' films rather than films that have serious storylines that discuss social and political issues. She believes that the major distributors and producers consider that audiences enjoy only films that have action or comedy. 'There are three taboos; sex, religion and politics,' Khalil says. 'You have to be conservative as a director, and as my films deal with social issues it is difficult with those taboos' (Monks, 2016). According to Khalil, censorship is a great barrier that directors must overcome and creative angles must be used in order to convey controversial storylines to pass censorship.

The Arab Spring era, proved to be advantageous as Egyptians gained more freedom for personal and creative expression, and women gained more rights and recognition. Films incorporated storylines that were important to society and a number of women's issues were featured. Although women still are a long way from equality, there is no denying that gender equality and women's rights in Egypt have significantly improved with each coming decade. Also, comedy and politics go hand-in-hand today as satire has become an important part of Egyptian pop culture. Egyptian films serve a purpose that is more than just delivering entertainment. The film industry in Egypt today tackles controversial, sensitive and alarming social issues that would often be overlooked or neglected by society, some of which are major issues that Egyptian women face on a daily basis.

CHAPTER 2

Her Story: Real and Reel

In the late 1800s and early 1900s, the regular role of Egyptian women in a family was that of a housewife. She did not leave her home without permission from the patriarch or question the system that limited her. However, Egyptian women expressed their frustration against gender inequality through political activism, which began in the revolution of 1919 (Ramdani 2013; p. 36). During the nationalist movement against the British in 1919, Egyptians of all classes including women joined the revolution.

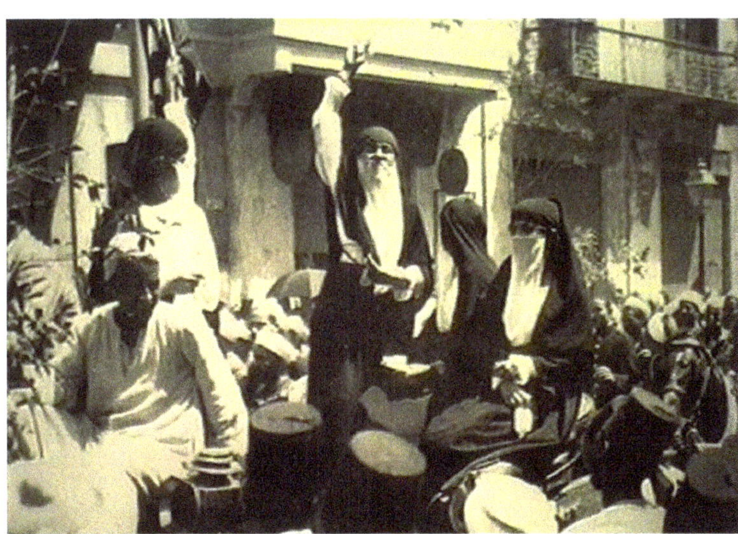

This image was taken during the 1919 revolution which saw women participate in demonstrations to remove British Rule from Egypt; women also demanded justice and gender equality

This was the first time that women would openly participate in a public rally. 'The veiled gentlewomen of Cairo paraded in the streets shouting slogans for independence and freedom from foreign occupation. They organized strikes and demonstrations, boycotts of British goods and wrote petitions protesting British actions in Egypt' (Marsot 1978; p. 269). These demonstrations were the crucible that birthed the feminist movement in Egypt.

Many women began using the publishing industry in order to express their dismay and voice their opinions to international audiences. In March of 1919, several petitions made by women were generated with titles that boldly identified them as citizens of the country like 'In the Name of the Women of Egypt,' and 'The Egyptian Women'. The petitions demanded liberation and equality for women in Egypt, after identifying themselves as 'Mothers of the Nation, and mothers, sisters and wives of the victims massacred for the satisfaction of British ambitions'. The movement ultimately turned into a women's demonstration in the revolution of 1919 calling for the removal of British occupation from Egypt and also highlighted the struggle of women in Egypt and the need for women's liberation (Ramadani 2013; p. 49).

The 1919 revolution was a watershed moment in the fight for freedom as Egyptian women broke cultural norms, challenged social and political authority, rallying on the streets united under the slogan 'Egypt for the Egyptians'. With both men and women joining forces, Egyptians managed to remove partial British control (with some contingencies attached) in 1922. By the mid-1920s, women demanded that nationalism and women's liberation should occur together in order for Egyptian society to progress. The 1920s proved to be a milestone as women began to challenge authority and break the shackles of cultural norms, which were often oppressive. While Egyptian men, in general, were unsympathetic to the idea of the women's movement, numerous women continued to rally for their cause creating their own power base (Ramadani 2013; p. 39). This struggle brought to the forefront many women of mettle who would change the destiny of their shackled sisters.

Breaking the shackles of patriarchy: Legendary feminists

One of the most prominent players in the fight for gender equality was Durriyyah Shafik, who founded the Egyptian women's organization, 'Bint-el-Nil' (Daughter of the Nile) in 1948.

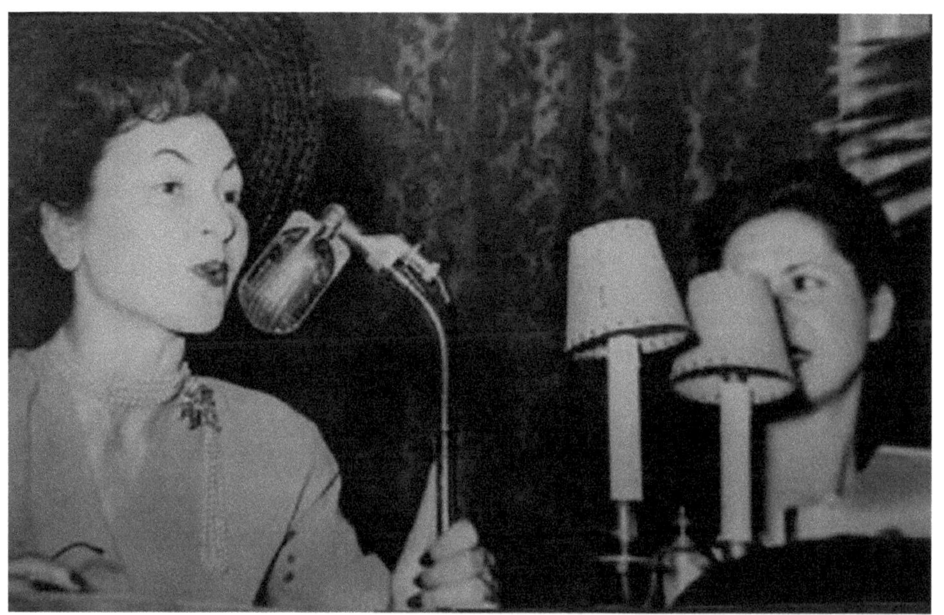

Feminist and activist Durriyyah Shafik spent much of her life fighting for equality for women. She was one of the leading feminists of Egypt and advocated for women's rights especially the right to vote.

Shafik was outspoken in her role as an activist and relentlessly fought for the rights of women of various social classes (Nelson 1996; p. 126). Though she was highly educated and received a doctorate in philosophy from the University of Sorbonne, she had a hard time finding a job upon her arrival in Egypt. Shafik was even rejected from a teaching position at Cairo University. As a middle-class citizen Shafik was convinced that Egyptian women could break the code of tradition only when they gained access to positions of decision-making within society. In order to do so, Shafik believed that women as legal citizens of Egypt needed to obtain the right to vote, in addition to gaining access to be nominated into the 'spheres of institutionalized power or the Parliament' (Khater 2002; p. 470). Articulate, highly educated, attractive, sophisticated and well dressed, Shafik was seen as the essence of the new Egyptian woman who emerged after World War II. Being the complete opposite of the traditional, secluded women of Egypt, Shafik focused her efforts on the elite sphere of male-dominated politics. She started off as an advocate of the upper class Egyptians and their right to be rulers of Egypt since she worked closely with Princess Shivakier and Princess Faiza on the establishment of the women's magazine *La Femme Nouvelle*. In the late 1940s, she stood for the middle class eventually considering them to be the most appropriate class to be rulers of Egypt (Khater 2002; p.470). As money and status were the privilege of the elite the only accessible route to power was through parliamentary politics, and Shafik focused on trying to open a path for women into politics. During this time, the 1952 revolution started. This would eventually demand the removal of the monarch, King Farouk, and would start the military reign in Egypt.

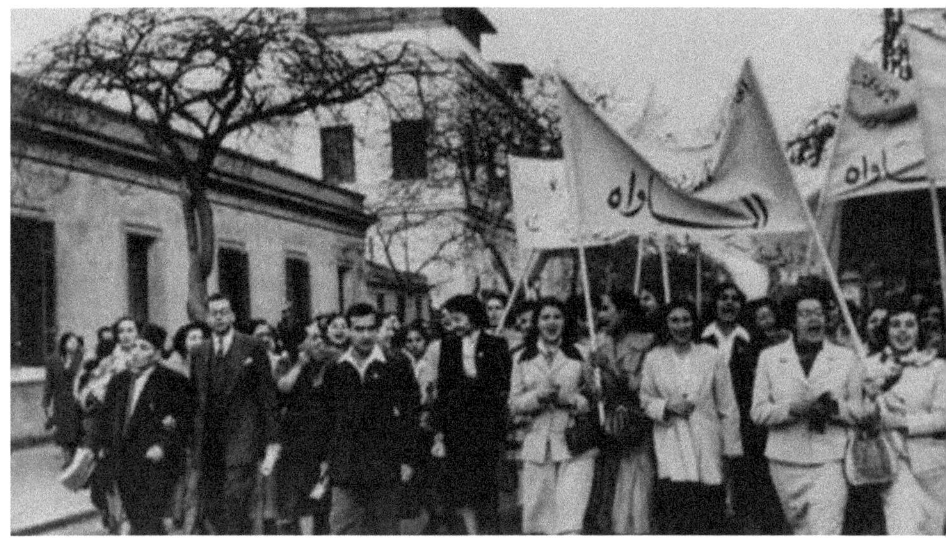

Durriyah Shafik (in the centre dressed in black) and the Daughters of Nile in a 1952 protest demanding political rights for women and inclusion of right to vote in the constitution.

It was around this time that Shafik demanded that educated women should have the right to vote and run for public office. Her tactics were staging demonstrations, writing newspaper articles, delivering lectures and carrying out hunger strikes with her colleagues, in order to acquire a seat in Parliament (Keddie & Baron 1991; p. 312). 'Durriya Shafiq led a large group of members of the *Bint el-Nil* association in storming the

Egyptian parliament to protest against the political exclusion of women from its membership' (Sparr 1994; p. 41).

In her magazine, *Bint-el-Nil*, Shafik shifted her focus from the 'old woman' to the 'new woman' of Egypt. This magazine focused on art, poetry, literature and culture, while her French magazine, *La Femme Nouvelle (The New Woman)* was targeted to the elite, bourgeois women, who she encouraged to become more liberal by dressing in affordable and elegant clothing, to follow dinner etiquette, to maintain a healthy youthfulness through exercise and to raise their children the modern (Western) way. The magazine advised the 'new' woman to also be aware of the political world. *Bint-el-Nil* did not directly focus on working women, addressing instead the stereotypical middle class women who were housewives and mothers (Khater 2002; p. 471). *Bint-el-Nil* played an indisputable role in spreading ideas.

The fight for constitutional reforms

In the late 1940s and early 1950s Egyptian middle class women became increasingly vocal about the importance of integrating women into different jobs as well as the political system from which they were excluded (Sparr 1994; p. 41). In 1950, Aisha Rateb, a lawyer, who later evolved to be a politician, minister, ambassador and professor, took legal action against the Ministry of Justice, which denied her a judge's job based on her gender. The Egyptian Feminist Union strongly supported Aisha Rateb in her fight for justice.

A number of feminist organizations continued to protest for women's rights throughout the revolution of 1952 which overthrew the monarchy that had ruled Egypt since the early 19th century. Although hesitant to abide by the feminist agenda that was presented by the Egyptian women's movement, the new state began to recognize that by integrating women in different platforms, they would be differentiated from the old regime. This idea helped the state to progressively move forward and award rights for women (Sparr 1994; p. 41).

Thanks to the efforts of Aisha Rateb and other vocal feminists, in 1956, a new constitution was born and women finally received the right to vote, work outside the home and acquired the right to an education at all levels. In 1959, Law 91 required employers that had more than 100 employees to offer female workers with social services which included daycare services and a paid hour on each workday to breast-feed their infants (Sparr 1994; p. 42). Working women were also given the right to maternity leave for 50 days and paid 70% of their salary. This rule came with the condition that the female worker had been employed for a minimum of 6 months. This was a huge fillip to working women across Egypt, who had been looking for equal opportunities in the workforce.

Four additional principles of the constitution helped shape the state's outlook towards women. Rule 31 of the 1956 constitution stated that 'All Egyptian citizens were equal in the eyes of the law and that there would be no discrimination on account of gender, origin, language or creed' (Jumhuriyat Misr 1956, as cited in Joseph 2000; p. 48). The state also committed itself to treating all employees fairly in regards to work specifications such as work hours, wages, insurance benefits and vacations (Joseph and Nagmabadi 2005; p. 666). The constitution guaranteed that all Egyptians would have access to equal opportunity. Law 14 of 1964 guaranteed jobs in the state sector for all Egyptians who earned high school diplomas and college degrees (Handoussa 1988, as cited in Sparr 1988; p. 42). With the state being on the side of all Egyptians in the workforce, employment became a significant element of Egypt's development programs and women in the labour force increased drastically. In fact, from 1961 to 1969, women's presence in the labour-force increased by 31.1%. In 1961, 41% of the working women worked in agriculture, however, this figure decreased to 23% in 1969 (Sparr 1988, p. 42). The percentage of women working in the manufacturing sector then increased from 3.3% to 13.5%. They took on jobs such as weaving and spinning in the clothing and textile industry and worked also in the food industry and the chemical industry. In 1961 54.1% of working women were teachers, 22.2% were nurses, 47% were in transportation and communication and 3.5% were in administration. In 1969 half of the female labour force was employed in the social service sector (CAPMAS ND, as cited in Sparr 1988; pp. 42–43). Feminization in the workplace increased in the 1970s as the females employed in the state sector continued to rise (Sparr 1988; p. 43). Women became regarded as citizens with rights and employees who contributed to the state sector and gained respect in the eyes of the law.

Women's role in the Egyptian Uprisings of 2011 and 2013

Prior to the Tunisian and Egyptian revolutions, the under thirty-fives, who made up to 75% of the population of the MENA region, were mainly portrayed in government and academic circles as a 'passive generation'. They were considered a lazy generation that did not deliberate on important issues in society. Yet it was this very generation that initiated, retaliated and was in the forefront of the political revolution that challenged the oppressive, political system and the inescapability of the 'Old Order' (Herrera 2014; p. 3).

The inevitable 25 January 2011 uprising was a result of the frustration of young Egyptians who were looking for justice after years of political and social abuse. The revolution was spurred by the sudden rise to popularity in January 2011, of the Facebook fan page 'We are all Khaled Said'. It was originally created in 2010 in honour of Khaled Said, whose death sparked outrage and became one of the most symbolic faces of the Egyptian uprising. Said was a young man from Alexandria who was said to have been tortured and killed by undercover police officers. Promoted by his parents, Khaled Said's story made nationwide headlines and continued to gain popularity, eventually culminating in Egypt's most dynamic and significant youth movement in over half a century. By January 2011, the Facebook page gained massive support receiving millions of posts daily. The page eventually grew to have more than 390,000 members, '70% of whom were under twenty four years old and over 40% of whom were young women' (Herrera 2014; p. 4). Shortly after the Tunisian uprising took off, the 'We Are All Khaled Said' Facebook page prompted a revolution in Egypt known as the January 25 Revolution (Herrera 2014, p. 3).

Throughout the 2011 revolution to oust former president Hosni Mubarak and the uprising in 2012 and 2013 to remove then president Mohamed Morsi, Egyptian men and women united in Tahrir Square under a common goal. One of the major causes championed in the revolution was the fight for gender equality. Women from across the country gathered to protest for a number of reasons including, social liberation and gender equality. Women of different ages and backgrounds were at the forefront of the revolution, and their participation was deemed to be both powerful and momentous. Upon entering Tahrir Square, also known as Liberation Square, women became equal participants in the frontline of the protest alongside men.

The story of the blue bra is one of the most iconic and memorable moments of the 2011 revolution. A video emerged online showing a young woman being brutally attacked by military police in December 2011. The female protester lay on her back and two soldiers dragged her by her abaya (cloak) while a third soldier stomped her upper body. Her abaya was torn off exposing her bust and a bright blue bra. The video went viral and was carried by several media outlets across the world causing outrage. The blue bra became the symbol of brutality against women.

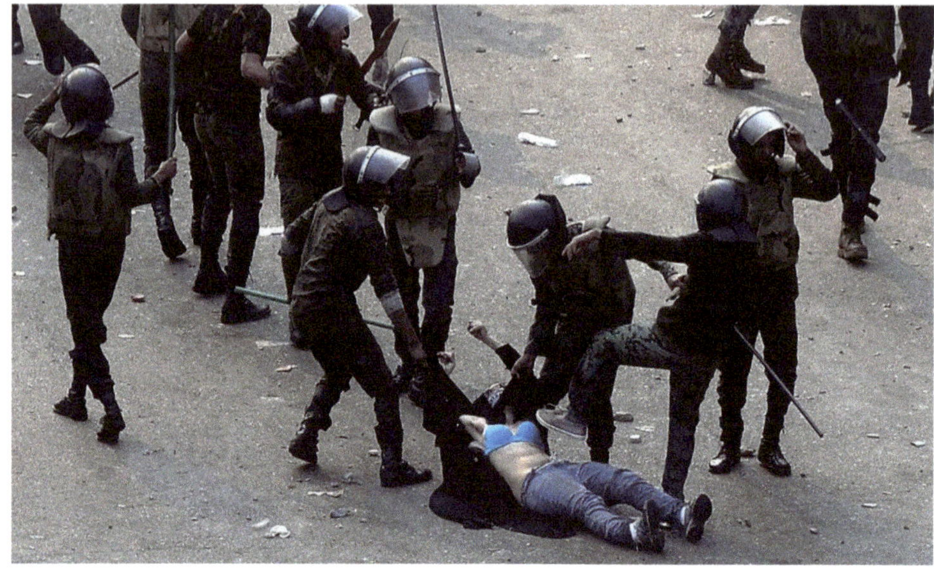

The blue-bra incident that evidenced police brutality against women protesters

The 2011 protestors used films, graffiti, photographs, poems, television programs and social media to express their opinions. Many online platforms including blogs, social media groups and websites advised women protesters specifically on self-defense and safety measures. This was to help women to protect themselves from possible mistreatment and violence from the all-male security forces and government-hired thugs, who were known to target women, unleashing physical and sexual assault (Kurtz and Kurtz 2015; p. 334). Women were advised to wear two layers of clothing and two headscarves to secure them well so as to prevent them from being torn off. Additionally, they were also warned against wearing clothing that had zippers and were encouraged to carry cans of mace. Egyptian journalist, Mona Eltahawy explains why these precautionary measures were essential for the protection of the female protesters. 'These young women were saying, "we will not be scared away. We are standing up for our rights to be active and equal members of Egyptian society"' (cited in Kurtz and Kurtz 2015; p. 334).

Violence and brutality against the protesters was the sole response from the military regime. Hundreds of people lost their lives and many thousands were injured turning the revolution to a bloody one. Violent reprisals from the government and military led the revolutionaries to believe that they were a long way from achieving democracy and reaching their ultimate goal of dignity for all. The protesters aimed to dismantle the political structure, which had kept the country in a state of emergency for over 30 years, and to put out of power a government which was deemed to be oppressive to all members of society, including women of all classes.

Aside from being leaders in the mass protest, women also volunteered to guard the entrance of Tahrir Square by conducting body checks on other female participants in order to ensure a peaceful and safe protesting space, a role that would have been culturally inappropriate for Egyptian men (Mekay 2011, as cited in Kurtz and Kurtz 2015; p.335). During the 18-day protest, women also set up temporary 'kitchens' and handed out food, water, blankets and medical supplies in the square (Saoub 2011, as cited in Kurtz and Kurtz 2015; p. 335). Furthermore, the women used tactics such as giving out flowers to security forces. As for the older women, they lived out their natural maternal roles hugging and kissing the soldiers. This was a powerful action as the identity of a mother 'has a significant cultural and political currency' and deliberately juxtaposes the feminine concept of 'motherhood and affection against the masculine concept of armed security forces' (Henderson and Jeydel 2007, as cited in Kurtz and Kurtz 2015).

By reaching out to soldiers and police forces of the Mubarak regime, the older women played a crucial role as mothers of the revolution communicating a message of acceptance and inclusion to the young men who were deemed to be enemies of the uprising. Women wanted to give the soldiers an opportunity to join the people and shift their loyalty and devotion from the Mubarak regime to the people's movement. The involvement of women in the revolution affirmed their status as Egyptian citizens. However, the use of gender tactics was imperative because they were able to strategically contribute to the movement in a unique way as women (Kurtz and Kurtz 2015; p. 335).

There is no doubt that this revolution, which will echo into the future, has addressed countless social and political issues on numerous fronts. Egyptians from all walks of life joined forces against the dehumanizing and unjust rule by a repressive regime. People participated in the attempt to oust the Mubarak regime in 2011, and the Muslim

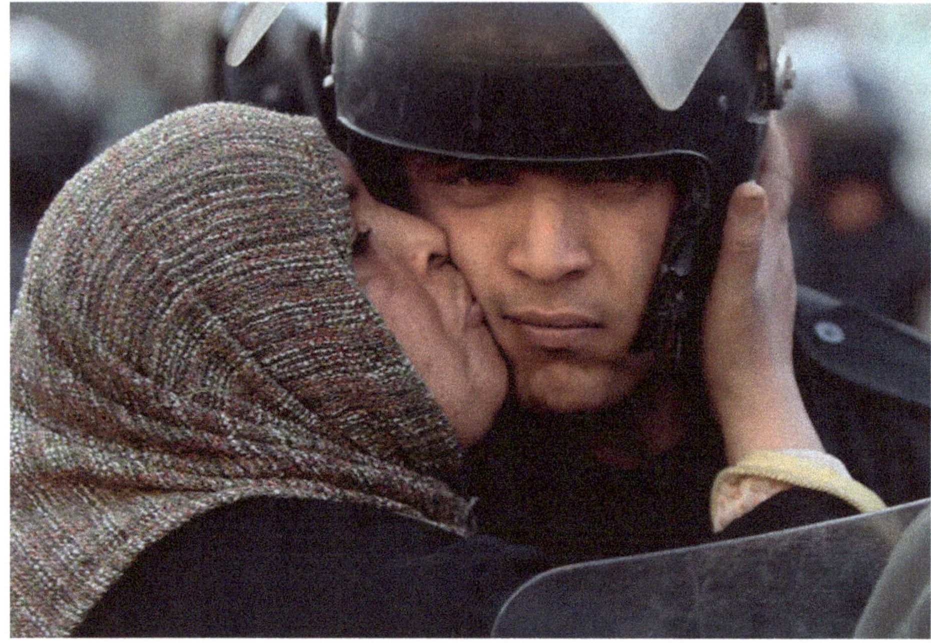

A powerful image of a woman protestor kissing a soldier deployed to oppress the protesters. This depicts the unique tactics that were used by women. Here they use their status as revered mothers to influence the young 'sons' to switch side.

Brotherhood in 2013. They came from completely diverse genders, affiliations, social positions, religions, cultures, and social class. The uprising became one that represented every single individual in Egypt. In spite of achieving political change in the aftermath of the revolution women were still excluded from positions of power. Though some rules have been implemented to curb sexual harassment against women equality is still a distant prospect. 'As witnessed in Egypt, in the post-revolution transition period, issues such as women's rights, equal political representation and family law are relegated to the feminine sphere and overshadowed by more important (i.e. masculine) causes such as national self-determination or democratic governance' (Chapple-Sokol et al. 2011; p. 109).

The use of social media enabled women to participate in and organize events connected to the revolution. The internet provided a platform for people to come together and share information which are crucial elements for political activism when faced with political repression, government censorship or when separated by geographical distance. Online communication and information sharing is often touted as a democratic, gender-neutral space where everyone's socioeconomic, cultural and gendered statuses exist on a level playing field. In fact, while there are many ways in which women gain access to new forms of power through their access to the internet, many if not most of the problems that women face in public offline spaces and communities exist in online spaces and communities as well, including barriers to internet access, oppression and harassment (Kurtz and Kurtz 2015; p. 335). Both offline and on line protest mechanisms mirrored gender segregation. 'The ways in which men and women participated in the protests, reflected the gendered dynamics of the Egyptian society, from the nationalist rhetoric that fueled the protests to the online and

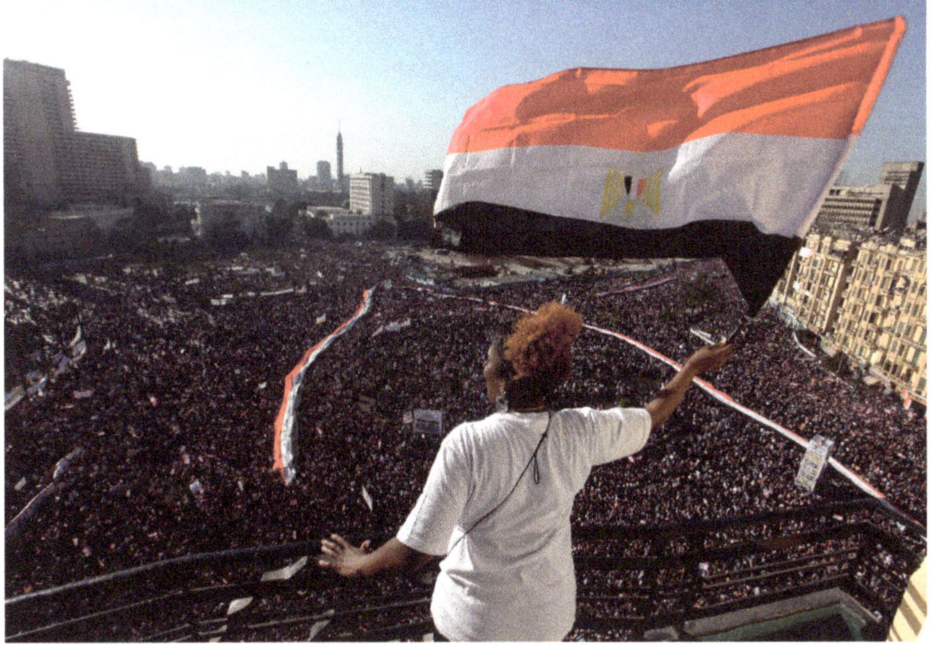

An Egyptian woman raises the national flag as she overlooks millions of people protesting in Tahrir Square.

physical spaces in which they operated and the non-violent strategic tactics they employed' (Chapple-Sokol et al. 2011; p 106).

Women's participation in the revolution was noticeable and the tenacity of women protesters of all ages proved that their impact was equal to that of men (Mostafa 2015; p. 123). Yet, this role was not a new one for women. The role of women in political life has dated back to the late 19th century. University of New York Professor Dr. Beth Baron believes that women who engage publicly in the social and political spheres are important in any society. She writes on the role of women in Egypt's revolutions: 'three trends- secularist, modernist and Islamist- stood out' (Baron 1994; p. 189). She continues to mention the way in which women represented themselves. 'They perceived themselves as a vanguard and saw their movement as one that would touch all women: Egyptian, Muslim and Eastern' (Baron 1994; pp. 189–191). Baron stresses that women had played a vital role throughout the nationalist movements that have helped redefine the gender relations in Egypt (Baron 1994; p. 188).

Egyptian women have engaged in struggles to enhance their condition under many former presidents including Gamal Abdel-Nasser, Anwar Al-Sadat and Hosni Mubarak. They fought to change women's lot in both the private and public domains and to transform the patriarchal structure (Mostafa 2015; p. 125). As a part of this there were strong protests against domestic abuse of women and sexual harassment in the private and public spheres. In the 18-day-long 2011 revolution, Egyptian women reverberated the historical struggle for gender equality with renewed vigour. Egyptian feminism expert and University of Sydney professor, Dr. Lucia Sorbera (2014) observed the power of women during the 18-day protest and said 'young women activists are articulating new approaches to feminism, and the experience of the eighteen days in Tahrir Square has been crucial in developing a new awareness, and experiencing what they call "a personal revolution"' (Sorbera 2014; p. 68).

Women from across all classes of Egypt joined together to give impetus to the struggle. It was believed that such a movement, which included a strong female presence, was crucial to combat the 'masculine chauvinism' which the military regime of Egypt had been using to influence politics and culture (Mostafa 2015; p. 125).

Doors to permanent and lasting change started to open soon and included the drafting of a new constitution. Egyptian women's rights activist Hala Kamal affirms that 'drafting a new constitution is always a good sign of a new political era in Egypt' (Mostafa 2015; p. 126). In January 2014, Kamal was involved in the process of formulating a

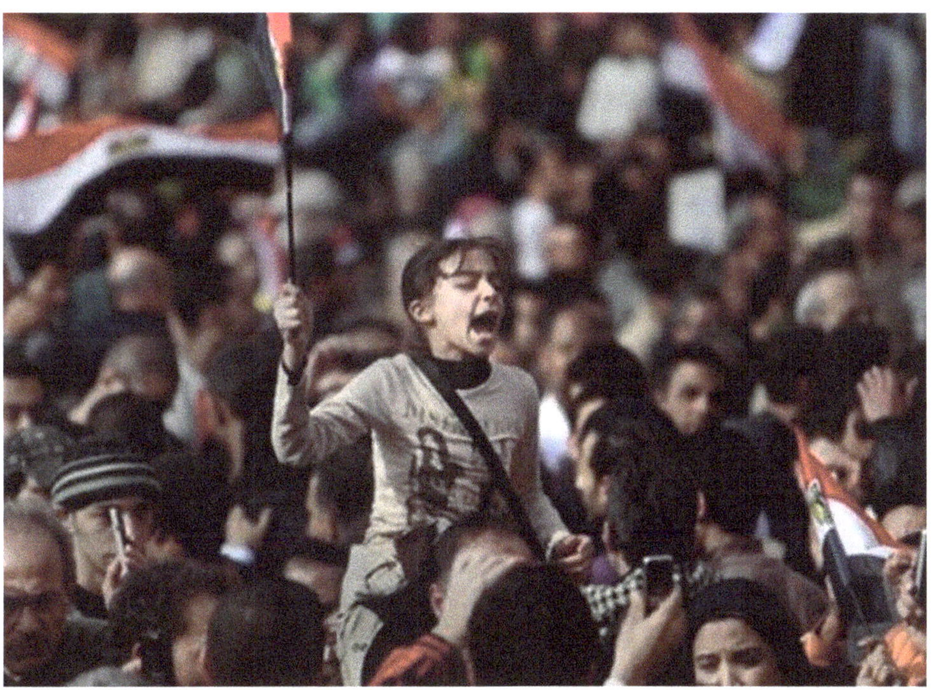

A young girl participates in the protests during the 2011 revolution. The revolution was inclusive and gathered people united by the same vision regardless of sex, age, religion or culture.

women's rights agenda and she negotiated to have it implemented in the new Egyptian constitution. She remembers the long and tedious journey endured in order to enact the change to the constitution: 'History has taught us in Egypt that ratifying a new constitution is not the end, but in fact the beginning of a new chapter of struggle' (Mostafa 2015; p. 126).

Women on screen: victims of the patriarchal construct

As cinema mirrors the socio-cultural discourse, it can throw light on gender and family relations in the nation. For years, Egyptian cinema has expressed and documented the changing circumstances and conditions of Egypt's history. Film served a great purpose as it gave insights on how the culture identifies itself through different situations (Ateya 2014; p. 62). It also helps to trace the changes to the female identity throughout the years.

Reem Obeidat (2002), an Arab media expert, believes that Arab media as a whole, is responsible for the way in which women have been perceived. She argues that Arab media has been indifferent about promoting a balanced image of women in society and favour the traditional role of women. Arab media should promote women's rights in a realistic way that touches on a range of issues from violence against women, equality before the law, women's education rights and more (Obeidat 2002; p. 4). Despite the fact that satellite exposure has assisted in the adoption of Western values and behaviours, society has not been receptive as the Arab-Islamic society is very protective of its traditions and cultural values. However, a number of popular Arabic movies that portray women in scenes of sex, violence and misogyny are broadcast to entertain Arab society though not in accordance with Islamic values (Obeidat 2002; pp. 2–3). This once again demonstrates how the Arab media misrepresents women. Additionally, Arab media focuses on female singers and superstars and fails to give attention to other leading achievers in society such as diplomats, teachers, lawyers, researchers and physicians. As a result, it fails to show responsibilities of men and women as equal, and fails to identify a number of strong and significant achievements of women in society (Ateya 2014; p. 64).

Several studies have analysed the depiction of female characters in Egyptian film. An extensive comparison of the images of men and women portrayed in Egyptian cinema was made by Nahed Ramzi a Researcher at Egypt's National Centre of Criminal Studies. Ramzi (1995) claimed that Egyptian cinema portrayed women negatively as those incapable of taking successful decisions in their family life and any decisions that they made always seemed to have a negative outcome for their family and marital lives.

Citing the Arab Development Report (2005), Ateya (2014) writes that in his book, *Surat al-Mar'a fi al-Masrah wal-Sinima* (*The Image of Women in Theatre and Cinema*), Samir Farid studied the images of women as portrayed in 410 Egyptian films that were produced between the years 1962 to 1972. His study showed that 44% of female characters were portrayed as unemployed (Arab Development Report 2005 cited in Ateya 2014; p. 64).

Dr. Mona El Hadidi (1977) conducted a study of films produced from 1962 to 1972, and analyzed 410 films and 460 female characters. El

Hadidi concluded that Egyptian cinema publicized a distorted image of women, showing them as depraved in their behaviour and/or in their thinking. Thus the portrayal of women continued to be that of sex objects as if following a set agenda. Rural women were under represented on the big screen and appeared in only 5.4% of the studied films. The study also showed that 22% of women were portrayed as housewives, while 20.5% were portrayed as employed women (El Hadidi 1977 as cited in Ateya 2014; p. 64).

The image of women in cinema from 1940–60 has almost always been that of submissive individuals who bear the pain of their families, and are completely compliant to those around them. The women's role symbolized the nation's values (Khatib 2006; p. 81). Examples of this can be seen in the 1996 film titled *Nasser 56*, which tells the life of the late President Gamal Abdel Nasser of Egypt. The film represents Egypt as a conservative and noble female, who does not pose a threat to patriarchy (Khatib 2006; p. 81). Although it was filmed in 1996, the film represented the ideal Egyptian woman during the 1950s, right at the centre of the Golden Age of Egyptian Cinema. The majority of Egyptian films from the 1940 to 1960s showed women as 'bearing the burden of being 'mothers of the nation" (Kandiyoti 1994; p. 376). Women are seen as fragile, loyal, obedient companions to their husbands and remaining in the private sphere. Family honour and national honour were considered the most significant ideals a wholesome Egyptian woman should cherish. This varied expectation argued that the mother's passion for her children can be a "safe' location of female desires'(Kaplan 1992; p. 79). The same author mentions that women who sacrifice for their husbands and families are seen as strong, heroic and innocent, 'she has ceased to be a threat in the male unconscious' (Kaplan 1992; p. 124). Such a paradigm 'uncritically embodies the patriarchal unconscious and represents woman's positioning as deficient, absence, signified and passivity' (Khatib 2006; p. 81) .

This concept can be seen in *Nasser 56* when Nasser's wife Tahiyya is presented as a self-sacrificing mother and devoted wife, who lives to take care of her children and husband, as she makes personal sacrifices for the sake of the nation. The end of the film shows Nasser on his deathbed, with Tahiyya beside him, saying 'it is only now that I have you for myself'. Such a statement confirms the sacrifices that Tahiyya makes for the well-being of the nation, which gives her a patriotic status (Khatib 2002; p. 82). The heroic status of Tahiyya was maintained throughout the film as she portrayed the role of an obedient wife, who complies with her husband's wishes. Her role as a housewife and hostess is seen as a commendable and expected trait in all Egyptian wives. Her obedience and capabilities as a hostess is depicted when her husband invites the Deputy Supreme Commander of the Armed Forces, Abdel Hakim Amer for dinner. The scene begins with a shot that reveals a long dinner table filled with food that Tahiyya cooked. As Nasser, Amer and Tahiyya sit at the table, the men compliment her culinary skills, after which she escorts them to the living room and serves them tea. Once the men begin to talk about politics, Tahiyya quietly excuses herself, saying that she must look after the children, and removes the sugar bowl from the tray commenting that she cannot trust her husband with sugar (Khatib 2002; p. 82). It is heart-warming that even as she excuses herself from a conversation that is deemed too serious for her, she still worries about the well-being of her husband.

Another image used to describe women is that of the mother of the nation. This is quite symbolic to Egypt because it represents a woman who has the ability to be gentle enough to look after the family in a loving and nurturing way yet is strong enough to sacrifice her family to protect the country's honour. Being a mother and being a woman is something that is considered profoundly sacred in Egypt. Interestingly, Egyptians identify Egypt itself as both a woman and a mother and refer to their country as 'Masr om el donia' which literally translates to: Egypt the mother of the world.

Representation of Egyptian women as patriotic heroines

Women have been filmed in their patriotic best in anti-Israeli films. Egypt has had a long and checkered history with Israel (Hirsh 1995). Parts of Egypt were annexed by Israel in 1967 and returned to Egypt in 1989 (Khatib 2006; p. 43).

In the 1990s, Egyptian cinema focused on producing films that highlighted the Israeli–Arab conflict. The films always portrayed Israel as an aggressor, and Palestinians as both the victims who lost land and the persistent resisters against Israel (Khatib 2006; p. 44). Egyptians have a strong connection to the Arab identity, thus, Egyptian cinema remained unsympathetic with Israel by continuing to portray Israel as a villain.

While the Egyptian cinema portrayed Israel as the enemy, Egyptian women were shown as triumphantly conquering Israel. However, while women played the roles of heroines, they were also forced into their traditional gender roles as well as sexually provocative ones like that of a seductress or a butch. Strengthening this argument, author Jack

Franco demonstrates how Egyptian films represent politically active women as 'performing limited acts of resistance'. He mentions films like *Al Tareeq ila Eilat* (*Road to Eilat*), which shows an Arab-led coalition, under the Egyptian marines on a secret mission in Israel. Amongst the troops are female fighters who are determined to aid Egypt in the 1973 October war against Israel, by going as undercover spies and assuming roles as sex baits. The women's roles were to seduce the Israeli men at the border, in order to gain access into Israel and gather intelligence (Franco 1994; p. 366).

This is not the only film that represents women in overtly sexual roles. This pattern is common and women's sexuality is often exploited. In the film '48 Hours in Israel', the Egyptian heroine worked as a show girl. In *Mohema le Tel Aviv* (*Mission in Tel Aviv*) the female character plays the role of a pro-Israeli spy, who uses her physical attractiveness to meet her ends. She uses her body and dance moves to sexually manipulate her enemies (Khatib 2006; p. 98). However, Egypt itself is represented as a sophisticated, modest woman, who obeys the patriarch and defends the family and country's honour (Khatib 2006; p. 81). Gender relations scholar, Denise Kandayoti (1994; p. 377) argues that 'women's appropriate sexual conduct often constitutes the crucial distinction between the nation and its other'.

Political films portraying Islamic fundamentalism

Egyptian political films have often represented active women who symbolize the modern face of Egypt (Khatib 2006; p. 11). However, the majority of films showcased the ideal wife as silent, veiled and obedient – a portrayal of the fundamentalist world view. Women are represented as repressed under the Islamic fundamentalist view, which is not a reflection of modern Egyptian women and the politically active women who abound in modern Egypt (Khatib 2006; p. 64).

In political films such as, *Al Akhar* (*The Other*, 1999) and *Al Irhabi* (*The Terrorist*, 1994), women are portrayed as silent, obedient and veiled and repressed by their Islamic fundamental husbands (Afshar 1996). The extent of the wives' obedience can be seen in the film *The Terrorist*, where Ali, a terrorist knocks on the door of his leader Ahmad's house. In that first shot, Ahmad is seen eating with his four chador-wearing wives. Once Ali knocks on the door, Ahmad dismisses his wives with a hand wave. In this scene, it is evident that the women are resigned to their place in the patriarchal hierarchy (Khatib 2006; p. 90). The veiled wives of the Islamic fundamentalists are unlike the regular women who are commonly seen in Egypt with casual clothes, jeans, make-up and a head scarf. Their clothing lacks colour, character or uniqueness. Throughout the history of Egyptian cinema (until recent years), it was widely recognized that overtly covered women would be connected to oppression.

By focusing on the obedient, oppressed wives of the typical fundamentalist, Egyptian films also tend to show the hypocrisy of society. In the movie, *Al irhab wal kebab* (*Terrorist and Kebab*, 1993), actress Yousra plays the role of a call-girl, a sensational woman with big hair, a lot of jewelry, heavy make-up and a revealing red dress. She does a short dance number to some cabaret music as she waves the frills of her dress and continues to walk down the stairs. The call-girl is an example of cinema's tempting, depraved harlot, who personifies the 'men's suppressed desires, and is a (sexual) object for the men's gaze, both in the film and in the audience' (Khatib 2006; p. 87).

After the initial stairway scene, the call-girl is seen speaking to Ahmad, an ordinary citizen who inadvertently started a protest against the government in a 13-storey government complex. Ahmed accidentally holds people hostage and demands justice for the people, including his hostages. He is not a villain in this movie and is liked by all the hostages. When Ahmad asks the call-girl why she chose to join the protest, she replies, 'I am too shy to say,' to which Ahmad responds, 'Do you feel shy like we do?' (Khatib 2006; p. 87). Ahmad's response symbolizes the call-girls 'essential otherness' (MacCabe and Mulvey 1989; p. 57) and the idea that as a call-girl she is shameless and sinful. The film thus affirms that simple women can be labeled as sinful and evil based on their appearance and their own sense of individuality.

The call-girl plays a significant role in identifying Rashad one of Ahmad's hostages as a hypocritical man whose desires lead him to be enchanted by the call-girl, his eyes nearly popping out on observing her breasts. Rashad advises the call-girl to follow the righteous path saying, 'All you need is a long dress and a veil and you will be virtuous.' The veil therefore becomes a metaphor for modesty in Rashad's view. His own passionate reaction is condoned. The call-girl's role in the film goes beyond that of a sexual object and is used to reinforce Egypt's morality which is in 'opposition to the corruption of Islamic fundamentalism' (Khatib 2006; p. 169).

Feminine metaphors representing space

Cultural studies scholar Hamid Naficy (1996; p. 128) believes that indoor and outdoor space is used in films to portray elements of nationalism. The nation itself is referred to as 'mother of the world,' a feminine and expansive term. The films that represent Egypt, are traditionally identified as feminine and there is an emphasis on interior spaces making the characters in the films less mobile than those in Hollywood films (Naficy 1996; p. 127). In several films, the physical 'outdoor' space of Cairo appears to be enclosed, with narrow interlocking winding roads and a womb-like structure that is meant to portray the safety and protection of people who live in the city. However, the 'symbolic agency that controls this space is clearly masculine' (O'Healy 1999; p. 254).

Naficy (1996; p. 128) argues that internal spaces can be seen as confining yet comfortable, which is often applied to the representation of Islamic fundamentalism in films. Fundamentalists are usually seen in confined, sheltered spaces away from a society that does not normally accept them as members of the community. In films such as *Al Irhabi* (*The Terrorist*), for example, Ali, the main character, lives in a minimalist and confined space, where a small bed, a rug and a light bulb hang from the ceiling, and, the overall ambiance of the room is dark and cold. The space thus isolates him from the outside world, and he is denied the shelter of the 'womb' of the capital city, Cairo (Khatib 2006; p. 34). At the same time, Ali's space is considered as a shelter that isolates him from the sinful pleasures of society. An example of space as an evil entity is seen when Ali walks through the streets of Cairo, where different colours are visible and human interaction with street vendors, neighbours and friends are part of the culture, that he is silently rejected from (Pidduck 1998). Feeling like an intruder in his own city, Ali makes his way back to his 'cocoon'. As he enters his house, he glances through the blinds of his window at the sounds and colours of the outside world. The space between the window blinds thus becomes Ali's only access to the outside world and its pleasures. Ali uses this space to glance at his neighbour, a beautiful woman, wearing a bright red dress. Ali fantasizes about the woman, making the woman part of the outside space, which he is denied.

Representation of females 1990 to present

During the boom in Cairo's construction industry, the capital city began to build malls which contained spacious and advanced movie theatres.

The cinemas showed both Egyptian and Hollywood releases. The industry's decline in the 1990s was reversed with the musical comedy *Ismailia rayeh gai* (*Ismailia Coming and Going*) by Karimi Dia Eddin in 1997 (Ginsberg & Lippard 2010; p. 126). The film, which was screened across Egypt, featured famous Egyptian comedian Mohamed Henidi. The film gained a massive fan base, and the comedy genre is still considered one of the most popular genres. The legendary Egyptian comedy star Adel Imam also helped to garner appreciation for comedies. From then, Egypt continued to lead the Arab world with many 'homegrown' film-makers and cast who have been trained through the Cairo Higher Cinema Institute (Armes 2015; pp. 8–9).

Women were seen playing more active roles in society on the big screen, and finally, in the next decade, the cinema began to see women flourish outside their stereotypical roles as obedient housewives, and as members of society.

In the mid-2000s, the Moroccan film industry began to thrive, but was unable to successfully surpass the popularity of the Egyptian film industry. The reasons for Egypt's continuing dominance in the film industry in the Middle East are varied. One reason could be that Egypt simply produces more films. For example, in 2007, Egyptian film-makers released 35 feature films, whereas Morocco produced 22 films in that same year and an additional ten films were produced across the whole of the Middle East. Additionally, Egypt is said to be the only country in the region that does not need state-aid, foreign co-production, or external funding for its locally produced films, as it has enough home based audience to make them commercially viable (Armes 2015; p. 9).

Egyptian films of this period represent women in a variety of roles. Depending on the genre and the context of the film, a woman could be portraying the role of a harlot, a strong female leader, a criminal, a housewife and more. A number of studies have been conducted on the representation of women. Jehan Yousry (2002) conducted a survey of 400 female college students from five different universities, in order to understand their perception of the image of women as seen in Egyptian films. Yousry's survey concluded that the students felt a lack of presence of rural and Bedouin Egyptian women and the problems that they face. Additionally, 63% of the participants believed that Egyptian cinema has failed to represent and tackle important women's issues. They also believe that the depictions of women in the films are far from reality. Earlier studies had come up with the same conclusions about under representation and misrepresentation of women in Egyptian films.

Another study was carried out to analyze the portrayal of women in Egyptian films from the year 2000. The study concluded that a number of women portrayed in these films are seen as indifferent about their educational status and most of the films in the study showed women of high economic status 'at the expense of those who belong to the middle and lower economic classes'. Other observations were that the portrayal of the women did not reflect reality and presented them as housewives who were religious, kind and loving, ignoring their aspirations and ambitions or need for self-fulfillment (Agwa 2000, as cited in Ateya 2014; p.65).

In the 2000s, there were attempts to portray women as strong, social individuals seeking equality and justice though this was not the norm. The Egyptian cinema of the new millennium increasingly began to depict women as successful, self-confident, forward thinkers, while some men have been portrayed with softened and sentimental features (Zeitoun 2005). The new era of Egyptian cinema took into consideration the women's rights and status quo in Egypt, by capturing the achievements of women.

The portrayal of women as strong, social individuals seeking equality and justice is notable in the 2007 film *Ehky ya Shaherzad* (*Shaherzad, tell me a story*), which sends the message that the only way women can free themselves from oppression is to face the fear of scandal and oppression head on. *Shaherzad, tell me a story*, is a powerful Egyptian film that outlines misogyny and overturns Egyptian stereotypes through the eyes of different women who come from various walks of life. The film is set in a television studio, in which television talk show host Heba (played by Mona Zaki), discusses current issues and scandals amongst women from across the country. The film focuses on terrorism, unemployment, corruption, assault, domestic abuse and oppression amongst women. Despite indirect threats from the government asking her to stop airing these issues, Heba continues to broadcast stories from different women whose lives are a representation of the current (and often graphic) social affairs in the country. The film comes from the works of auteur directors Yousry Nasrallah and Waheed Hamed, who are known to tackle modern issues in their work. Referring to the issue of domestic violence Zaki said, 'women are being beaten and oppressed all over the world. The film *[Ekhy ya Shaherzad]* received an eight-minute standing ovation at the Venice Film Festival. People were crying and saying you are talking about something that touches women globally' (The National, 2009).

Interestingly, the film received much criticism after it was released. It was attacked for showing sexual behaviours and sexual and domestic abuse. Seeing such graphic scenes that mirrored reality on screen, was a shock for many – both men and women, who were unable to handle such overt sexual imageries (Collette-White 2009). However, Zaki defended the role stating, 'the men behind this kind of treatment are worried that women seeing this film will rise up and say, why not all of us? The point is that there are people who want to go back to the dark ages. They are becoming more and more visible in our world. And me being an actress, a well known actress, I might affect a lot of women who will see it' (*The National* 2009). Women and their sexuality are commonly featured in the film industry regardless of the backlash. Similarly, many films continued to outline and challenge the fundamental flaws that have been normalized by society. 'Film-makers now a days seek to deepen the discourse on women through studying the complex mechanisms of the relations between the genders and trying to bring it to the surface' (Ateya 2014; p. 62).

Today, the film industry continues to thrive and covers political and social issues. Many of the Golden Age stars maintain their relevance, as they are remembered on social media. Their films are regularly aired on Egyptian satellite television channels, some of which are strictly dedicated to classic Egyptian cinema (Armes 2015; p. 9).

CHAPTER 3

Iconoclasts: Representation of Women in the Golden Age of Egyptian Cinema

As reported by various academic studies that have attempted a content analysis of films of both eras, Egyptian films in general do not represent the bold women who emerged during the freedom struggles. Hence, the films analysed in detail have purposefully been chosen to showcase the strong female ethos.

To compare the reel roles and real life roles of women, twenty Egyptian films were observed. The films were selected based on the choice of actresses and the plot which had a storyline that focused on women. The actresses were an important focus when selecting the films because of their influential profile both on screen and off screen. In addition to this the message that they deliver through their characters and how strongly they play the role to portray their reality as everyday women in a patriarchal regime were considered. First, ten films from the Golden Age era were selected and analyzed based on the plots, role of main female characters, their level of education and employment status, goals and accomplishments and mannerisms and lifestyle.

The films that were selected from the Golden Age era for review were released between the years 1950 to 1966. This study features the films: *Al Avocato Madiha* (*Madiha the Lawyer*), *Al Ostaza Fatma* (*Mrs. Fatma*), *Raya wa Sakina* (*Raya and Sakina*), *Banat Hawa* (*Eve's Daughters*), *Al Anessa Hanafi* (*Miss Hanafi*), *Ana Horra* (*I'm Free*), *Sayedat Al-Qasr* (*Queen of the Castle*), *El Bab El Maftouh* (*The Open Door*), *Lel Regal Fakat* (*For Men Only*) and *Meraty Modeer Aam* (*My Wife the General Manager*).

The following table represents the characteristics of the main female character(s) of the Golden Age films that were analyzed for this particular study.

Film	Year of Release	Profession	Social and Political Activi
Golden Age of Egyptian Cinema			
Al Avocato Madiha *Madiha The Lawyer*	1950	Lawyer	Yes
Al Ostaza Fatma *Mrs. Fatma*	1952	Lawyer	Yes
Raya wa Sakina *Raya and Sakina*	1953	Thieves	No
Banat Hawa *Eve's Daughters*	1954	Manager	Yes
Al Anessa Hanafi *Miss Hanafi*	1954	Unemployed	No
Sayedat Al-Qasr *Lady of the Palace*	1958	Unemployed	No
Ana Horra *I am Free*	1959	Project Manager	Yes
Al Bab Al Maftouh *The Open Door*	1962	Student	Yes
Lel Regal Fakat *For Men Only*	1964	Engineers	Yes
Meraty Modeer Aam *My Wife the General Manager*	1966	General Manager	Yes

Level of Education	Physical Appearance		Lifestyle	
	Clothing	Hijab	Alcohol	Breaks Taboos
Has a degree	Western	No	Yes	Yes
Bachelor's Degree	Western	No	Yes	Yes
Uneducated	Traditional Egyptian galabeyas	Yes	Yes	Yes
Bachelor's Degree	Western	No	No	Yes
Unknown	Western/galabeya	No	Yes	No
Unknown	Western	No	Yes	No
Bachelor's Degree	Western	No	No	Yes
Bachelor's Degree	Western	No	No	Yes
Has a degree	Western/Masculine	No	No	Yes
Master's Degree	Western	No	Yes	Yes

An in-depth analysis of individual films is added below to help understand their context and role of female characters.

Al Avocato Madiha (Madiha the Lawyer)

This 1950 film revolves around a strong headed woman whose ultimate goal is to become a well-known lawyer. After leaving her village for a few years to study in Cairo, Madiha returns to her home and discovers how different her mentality is in comparison to those around her. Back in her village, she experiences culture shock, as her family and the rest of the village celebrate traditions that are different from what she is familiar with in Cairo. Her family is surprised when they discover that Madiha's ideas and way of life are very different from that of the villagers. Aside from refusing marriage, Madiha is also against staying home and doing housework and is determined to become a prominent lawyer. Her family struggles with understanding her ideas as she pursues her career goals and lives her life independently, without consideration for her heritage, family and traditions.

Madiha is an educated woman with big career plans that will be put on hold due to culture or a patriarchal regime that will get in the way of her dreams. She does not believe that women belong at home and rejects marriage. She is not afraid of being different or controversial and is a very well-spoken and assertive woman.

The most noticeable thing about this film is the way Madiha speaks with passion about her rights as a member of society. The main character, Madiha is played by actress Madiha Yousry, who has powerfully essayed several different roles in other films including that of a feminist who fights for her rights and breaks the cultural taboo.

Al Ostaza Fatma (Mrs. Fatma)

This film was released in 1952 and features Fatma, a smart girl who is a high achiever in her university. Fatma shows characteristics of a strong and confident feminist who prioritizes her education and career. She fights for women's equality and does not follow the patriarchal system and often disobeys her father. After graduating with a Bachelor's degree in law, she opens a law firm, but her fiancé Adel is envious of her success and does not believe in Fatma's abilities as she is a woman and being a lawyer is not a woman's profession. Angered by his comments, Fatma challenges Adel to a competition, which eventually becomes too competitive and drives the couple apart. Things take a turn for the worst when Adel gets falsely convicted of murder and asks Fatma to be his lawyer and prove his innocence. After winning the case, Adel accepts Fatma's career ambitions. Meanwhile Fatma decides that there is no case that she could ever get that would be as satisfying as Adel's case. Therefore, instead of continuing with her successful career, she decides that it is time for her to settle down and start a family.

Fatma has a strong passion for justice both in her professional and personal life. She embodies a woman who is not afraid to be a successful lawyer in an era that does not believe this to be a suitable career choice for a woman, so she is forced to prove herself to the people around her.

Raya wa Sakina (Raya and Sakina)

This 1953 horror thriller is based on the true story of Egypt's first and most notorious serial killers, real-life sisters Raya and Sakina. These sisters terrorized the city of Alexandria in Egypt in the 1920s by committing a series of murders in order to steal gold jewelry. Though several women in their community began to disappear without a trace, Raya and Sakina were never suspected. The criminal acts continued for two years before the police began to suspect the sisters. The evidence of the murders started to trace back to the sisters, whose strategy was to kidnap women who wore gold jewelry, in order to steal the valuables. The sisters would invite the women over to a party at their house, with the promise of a good time and alcohol. Once the women were inebriated, Raya and Sakina would ask their husbands to choke the women until they died and then bury them beneath their house. More than twenty women were killed in this manner. The story is widely circulated in Egypt, and many renditions of the murderous duo have been made in the forms of plays, films and television series.

This film revolves around two murderers who are both unemployed and uneducated, but they are determined women. They are strong willed and as such, their husbands are the ones that follow, while they plan, lead and execute. Their gang consisted of the sisters, their husbands and two other friends – all of whom followed the sisters' orders, particularly Raya's. Both Raya and Sakina come from extremely impoverished neighbourhoods. This is a deciding factor in the trajectory of the sisters' lives and differs from the rest of the films in the study.

Banat Hawa (*Daughters of Eve*)

This film is an adaptation of Shakespeare's *The Taming of the Shrew*. Released in 1954, this film features the story of two sisters who are complete opposites. One sister, Hekmat, is infatuated with the idea of falling in love and getting married, while the other sister, Esmat, has no interest in love, family or marriage because she is a strong, independent woman, who wants to work in the parliament. Hekmat does not like men and finds them to be misogynistic and inefficient. She starts her own organization for women and leads the group by spreading the word that men are incompetent and inadequate. She has dreams and aspirations of joining the parliament and doesn't believe that anything could stop her. By coincidence, she meets a man named Waheed. Waheed is cheesy and flirtatious, a perfect concoction of the kind of man that she would despise. However, there is no avoiding him, as he is always roaming around her workplace. Hekmat eventually takes matters into her own hands to get rid of him and she devises a plan to disassociate from him as she realizes that she is starting to like him. After denying it to herself and others, she eventually falls in love with Waheed and marries him.

Hekmat's character was one of the first of its kind in Egyptian cinema, as she was portrayed with strong aspirations to join the parliament – suggesting that women could and should be working in government bodies, which is something that was not common in Egypt in the 1950s.

Al Anessa Hanafi (*Miss Hanafi*)

This 1954 film was ahead of its time as it tackles more than one controversial issue. Hanafi and Hassan are both in love with Nawaem, and are trying to win her heart. Hanafi and Nawaem are step-siblings and live together as Hanafi's father is married to Nawaem's mother. Hanafi has a dictator-like personality, and he believes as a man he has power over a woman. He is very assertive in his home, and extremely oppressive towards the women in his life. He does not believe in women's rights and freedom and believes that women should not leave the house without permission. In addition to this, Hanafi has strong opinions about his step-sister's choice of clothing and is not shy to mention this. As a result, Nawaem and her mother are both miserable and spiteful towards Hanafi. Hanafi has made a set of rules that are repressive towards women in order to keep the control of the house in his own hands. When he suffers severe stomach pain, Hanafi is admitted into emergency surgery, where he accidentally receives a sex change operation. After his recovery period, Hanafi, now known as Fifi, comes home and tries to start her new life as a female (with masculine features). As she is now a new person, Fifi's personality has become the complete opposite of Hanafi's. Fifi is playful and flirtatious and does not believe that the oppression of the patriarch applies to her. She understands that being a woman in a man's world is hard but doesn't change her personality to play the part of the obedient Egyptian woman.

The most notable part of this story is the irony that Hanafi turned to Fifi and in turn understood the struggle of being a woman through personal experience. This film is a comedy and the character of Hanafi is played by Ismail Yassin, one of the most popular comic actors of the Golden Age era.

Sayedat Al-Qasr (*Lady of the Palace*)

This 1958 film features Adel, a wealthy playboy who spends his days drinking and gambling. He sets his eyes on Sawsan, a working-class orphan who does not approve of their relationship due to their societal differences. Eventually they get married and Sawsan witnesses Adel's troubling lifestyle. As she disapproves of his habits and his friends' behaviour, Sawsan is ordered by Adel to stay at home, while he goes out with his friends. Sawsan soon realizes that Adel owns a piece of land and she manages to get the documents only to find out from Adel's childhood friend that her husband is trying to sell the property. After discovering this information, she finds out that Adel's friends are exploiting him and stealing his money. Sawsan works against all odds to prove to her husband that his friends are not what they appear to be. This causes major problems between Adel and Sawsan, and she decides to leave once and for all. Eventually Adel discovers the truth about his friends and returns to his wife. He apologizes for his mistakes and assures Sawsan that he will change and give up his previous dishonorable lifestyle.

This film shows the heroine as the leading character. She is an astute woman, who is able to manage her life and their assets. Against all odds, she is able to successfully bring down a group of criminals which has been terrorizing her and stealing from her husband. The film shows how a woman's resilience and strength goes a long way and that it has the ability to change a man.

Ana Horra (*I am Free*)

Released in 1959, *Ana Horra* is a film that features Amina, a high school student in her senior year who is fed up of the patriarchal system in Egypt. Amina is living with her aunt, uncle and cousins as she tries to defy her male relatives who are restricting her from things she wants to do (work, go to university etc.). She is unable to cope with the double standards meted out to the men and women of society. Her main goal is to be able to do all that she desires without being judged and insulted due to her gender and the actions that she chooses to do as a woman. She feels that she does not need to answer anyone and she thinks that women are severely oppressed and are in denial of this fact. She is constantly defying the conservative traditions that oppress women in Egyptian society and fights against male dominance that attempts to restrict her from living her life on her own terms. She struggles with the idea that women should stay at home and obey their husbands and fathers. After continuously fighting with her family about her outgoing lifestyle, Amina enrols in university without anyone's consent and starts working in a company shortly after her graduation. She is so immersed in her work responsibilities that she soon begins to feel that she has lost all her freedom. In a strange coincidence, she meets her old neighbour Abbas, who is now an opinionated journalist. Amina begins to embrace Abbas' work and his political opinions, which she strongly agrees with. Eventually both Abbas and Amina get imprisoned for publicizing their revolutionary beliefs. They get released and get married and vow to continue to fight the system.

This film is unlike any other because even after the marriage, the female character continues her fight both in the personal and political realm. Her opinions and beliefs do not change because of her nuptials, rather, this lifelong commitment to her husband only makes her desire for change stronger.

Al Bab Al Maftouh (*The Open Door*)

This 1964 film showcases Laila, an independent woman who has strong opinions about the army and politics in Egypt. She struggles to accept societal norms that mandate a woman to become a housewife who takes care of her husband and children. Laila falls in love with her brother's friend who is away at war, but is forced by her parents to marry her university professor, Dr. Fouad, who has expressed interest in her because of her intellectual capabilities.

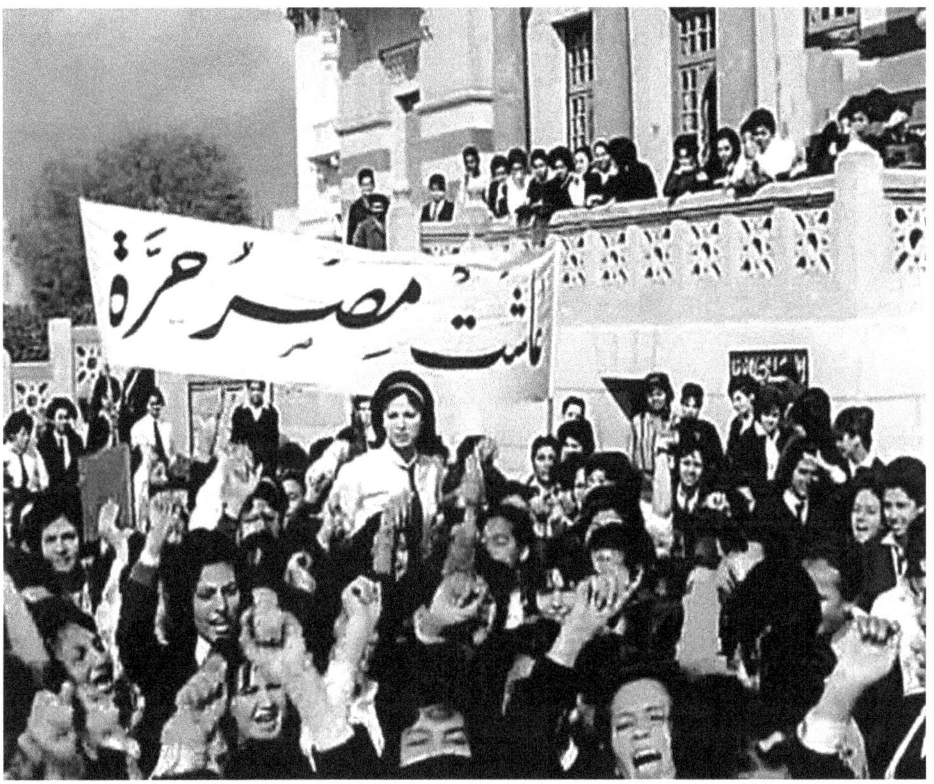

This scene from ***Al Bab Al Maftouh*** shows an independent and opinionated Laila leading a political protest, primarily comprising women from her university.

Laila's cousin Gamila advises Laila not to get married and submit to social pressures. Her advice comes based on her experiences, having endured a failed marriage that lasted only a week. Gamila's family had refused to go public with the divorce as it would bring shame and taboo to the family. After their wedding, Laila overhears Dr. Fouad saying that women should be obedient and loyal, and that Laila falls into this category, thus he expects her to be a great wife and mother who follows the patriarchal system and the expectations of Egyptian society. Offended by his words, she gives her wedding ring back to Dr. Fouad and follows her dreams of being with her boyfriend Hussein and being part of the movement against Israel. Laila is strongly against the political injustice that Israel has caused, therefore, when Hussein is set to travel back to Port Said to fight in the war, Laila follows him and eventually joins him. The film ends with them leaving to Port Said together; their fate is not portrayed in the film.

Lel Regal Fakat (*For Men -Only*)

Released in 1964, *Lel Regal Fakat* is about two female engineers, Elham and Salwa who have been working on a project from their office in Cairo in order to help produce gas in the middle of the desert. The girls propose an idea to their manager requesting to be sent to the desert, where the rest of the team is. This would be easier for the women and their work would be more efficient if they are on-site. The manager declines this request, stating that the work in the desert is a man's job and that as women they will not be able to handle it. Elham, furious about her manager's comments, convinces Salwa that they should dress as men and go to the desert anyway and work on the project from there. Reluctantly, Salwa agrees. The women dress up as male engineers and live amongst their male co-workers until they have successfully completed their project.

It goes without saying that their male counterparts are shocked at their success and their ability in spite of being women to work in the field. In the end the men admit that they did not know that women had the capabilities of working under harsh conditions and the lesson behind the film is made clear.

Meraty Modeer Aam (*My Wife is a General Manager*)

In 1966, *Meraty Modeer Aam* was released and challenged the male authority as the leader of the house. A married couple who have a great power balance at home find themselves in a situation where the wife, Esmat is the general manager of the company where her husband, Hussein works. Esmat was working in a different department of the same company, when she got promoted. It was not known to Esmat or Hussein that she would move to Hussein's department, thus, becoming his manager, to whom he would be reporting directly. Hussein's male colleagues are in a state of shock and disappointment upon discovering that their boss is a woman. As Esmat is a unisex name, the employees naturally assumed that their new manager was a man.

Embarrassed because he has to report to his wife, Hussein convinces Esmat to keep a low profile about their relationship and they go to

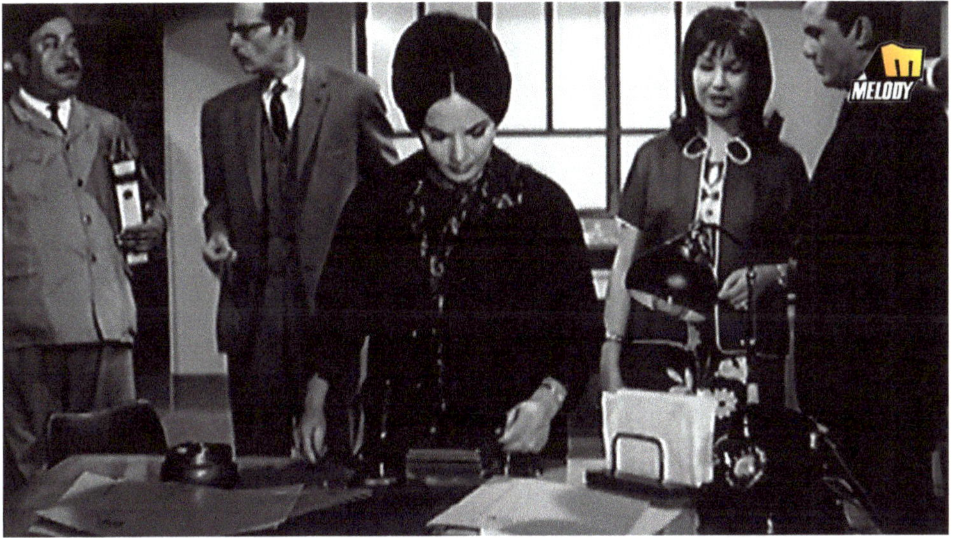

A scene from the movie *Meraty Modeer Aam* showing Esmat with her husband. Both work in the same company where Esmat is a manager and her husband reports to her.

extreme measures to ensure that their marriage remains a secret in front of their colleagues. As expected, the work becomes demanding and Esmat becomes assertive to Hussein causing a strain in their marriage and especially to Hussein's ego. Eventually, Hussein's colleagues learn that Esmat is his wife and manager, and the 'scandal' makes him the laughing stock of the office.

Esmat is a very professional individual who is always dressed in business attire with her hair tied back or in an up-do. At home her focus is to care for her husband and his happiness. She is a considerate wife and is very obedient as well as flirtatious at home. However, at work she is forced to be aggressive and dominant, considering that the majority of those who report to her are men. She feels the need to have to prove herself as a valuable and strong leader to a team comprised mostly of men, none of whom respect her as a leader, simply because of her gender.

This selection from the Golden Age of Egyptian Cinema shows women who are distinct from the average Egyptian housewife. These women characters fought to take up work outside of the home and get an education, and many are indifferent to love and marriage. They are unveiled, dressed in modest, western clothing and occasionally drink alcohol. The women had to struggle to step out of their homes and could never go unaccompanied though this is no longer an issue in Egypt today. However, with all the movies that were analyzed, love and marriage was the grand finale although how life after marriage evolves remains unclear. What is certain is that, despite the difficulties and the conservative views that were expressed all the women in the study proved to be successful leaders who managed to accomplish their main goals even when it was against the patriarchy. Some of them were involved in the fight for social justice, gender equality and political change. Interestingly, in Hollywood there were very few female-oriented movies made during this period and *Thelma and Louise*, heralded as iconoclastic and challenging traditional female roles, was released in 1991. The films studied here released between 1950 and 1966 have themes that were far ahead of their time and rare even in Western cinema. The social situation of the time had given birth to many women warriors who set out to change the lot of their sisters and also of their nation. This spirit is seen in the selected films too, mirroring the milieu of the period.

CHAPTER 4

Back to Bondage: Representation of Women in the Pre and Post Revolution Era of Egyptian Cinema

The Egyptian revolution which ousted former president Mohamed Hosni Mubarak began on 25 January 2011 and lasted eighteen days. This revolution did not happen impulsively. In fact, there are a number of films that expose the social and political corruption within the system, that led to the revolution. Many of these films feature both men and women fighting for their rights and working together for one common goal.

The films that were selected from the pre/post revolution era for review were released between the years 2005 to 2013. This was required to capture the social and political events that led up to the revolution and to evaluate its effects. The films reviewed are: *El-sefara fi El-Omara (The Embassy in the Building)*, *Heya Fawda* (*This is Chaos*), *Hassan wa Morcos* (*Hassan and Marcus*), *Welad el Amm* (*Escaping Tel Aviv*), *Ehky ya Shahrazad* (*Shahrazad Tell Me a Story*), *Cairo 678*, *Bentein Men Masr* (*Two Girls from Egypt*), *Asmaa*, *Fatat al Masna* (*Factory Girls*), *Teymour we Shafika* (*Teymour and Shafika*) .

The following table represents the characteristics that help identify the views and roles of the main female character(s) of the pre and post revolution films that were analyzed for this particular study.

Film	Year of Release	Profession	Social and Politica[l] Activism
Pre/Post Revolution			
El-sefara fi El-Omara *Embassy in the Building*	2005	University Professor	Yes
Teymour we Shafika *Teymour and Shafika*	2006	Ambassador	Yes
Heya Fawda *This is Chaos*	2007	Unemployed	Yes
Hassan wa Morcos *Hassan and Marcus*	2008	Unemployed	Yes
Welad al Amm *Escaping Tel Aviv*	2009	Unemployed	No
Ehky ya Shahrazad *Shahrazad Tell Me a Story*	2009	Television Host	Yes
Cairo 678	2010	Government worker, comedian, jewelry designer	Yes
Bentein Men Masr *Two Girls from Egypt*	2010	Doctor & administrator	No
Asmaa	2011	Office Worker	Yes
Fatat Al Masna *Factory Girls*	2013	Tailor	No

Level of Education	Physical Appearance		Lifestyle	
	Clothing	Hijab	Alcohol	Breaks Taboos
Has a PhD	Western	No	Yes	Yes
Has a PhD	Western and professional	No	No	Yes
Teacher, principle and home-maker	Western and galabeya	1 out of 3	No	Yes
Unknown	Western and religious attire	Yes	No	Yes
Unknown	Western	No	No	No
Unknown	Western	1 out of 3	No	Yes
Unknown; 1 out of 3 may not be educated	Western and Islamic	1 out of 3	No	Yes
Bachelor's Degree	Western	No	No	No
Uneducated	Islamic	Yes	No	Yes
Bachelor's Degree	Western	No	No	Yes

El-sefara fi El-Omara (The Embassy in the Building)

This pre-revolution film released in 2005 features a womanizer, Sherief Khairy, who returns to Egypt after living in the UAE for 25 years. He finds the Israeli embassy and the residence of the Israeli ambassador located next door to his apartment in Cairo. Sherief has a hard time adapting to his living situation as security screening measures have been implemented, for the safety of the residents of the building, and especially for the Israeli ambassador. Shortly after returning to his difficult living conditions, Sherief meets Dalia, a political activist who is determined to bring down the system that supports the values of Israel, which she and the general public deem to be cruel and unethical. These circumstances help change Sherief from a selfish misogynist with no views or political opinions, to an anti-Israel icon, supported by the community around him. With guidance and support from Dalia, Sherief leads rallies and protests to get justice for the people of Palestine.

The most significant aspect of this film is the fact that Dalia is not only leading all the protests and demonstrations, but she is also leading Sherief and teaching him about the oppression and driving his passion. Dalia is a political science professor and is highly educated. She is a modern woman with a very strong passion to fight for injustice. She is the main reason for his change and for the demonstrations that gather both men and women with a common belief. In some scenes Dalia is seen carried on top of a crowd as she leads the anti-political chants.

Teymour we Shafika (Teymour and Shafika)

Teymour we Shafika is a popular 2007 film and a classic example of the ever-changing system in Egypt today. Growing up together as neighbors and friends, Teymour and Shafika fall in love. However, their future is not as trouble free as all had expected, as their personalities mature and their career choices are made clear. Teymour is an image of the stereotypical, traditional Egyptian man with conservative ideals. He is dominating and controlling. His word is the final word and he is not open to compromises or discussions.

Shafika however, embodies the modern Egyptian woman. She is highly educated (with a PhD), ambitious, strong and open-minded. Through her hard work, Shafika becomes a minister while Teymour becomes her bodyguard. Their situation as co-workers and lovers take a turn for the worst when Shafika is unable to handle Teymour's closed-minded and demanding attitude.

The film portrays Shafika as a strong woman who holds a high position of power in the parliament. She has poise, elegance and is highly intellectual and represents the everyday Egyptian female, who fights for her career and her independence as a woman living in a man's world. The film shows that both Teymour and Shafika need each other for their professional advancement and that through compromise they can both achieve their goals and desires.

Heya Fawda (This Is Chaos)

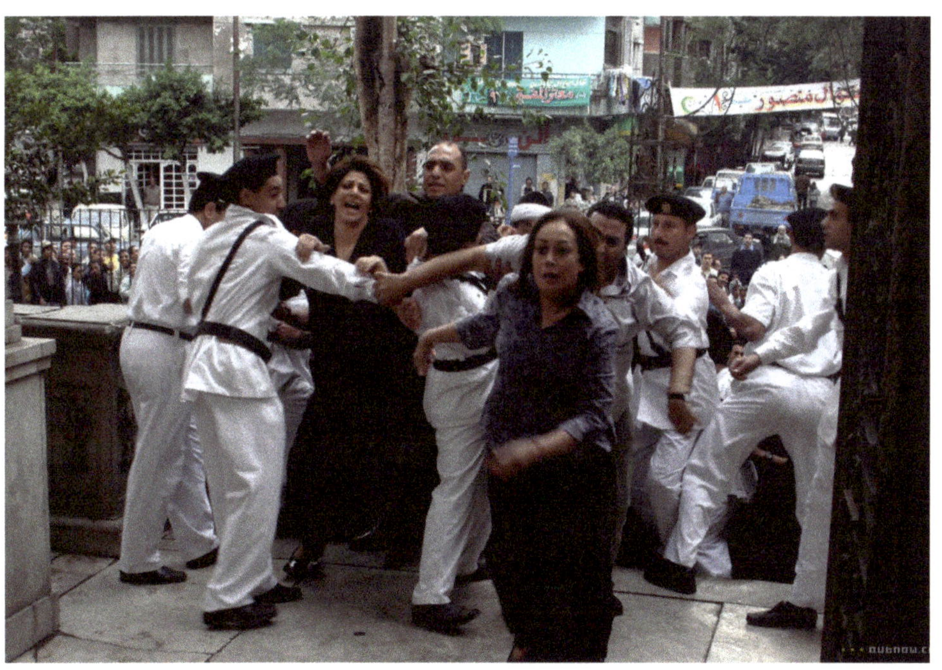

Heya Fawda is a movie that outlines police brutality and corruption. When Nour becomes the subject of harassment, assault and rape, her mother and friend lead a rally to get justice for her.

This 2007 film is mainly located in the popular neighborhood of Shobra in Cairo. Police officer Hatem handles the neighborhood with an unjust iron fist. All the members of this neighborhood fear Hatem as he is brutal and evil, and justifies all his actions with his status as a police officer who works for the system. Nour, his neighbour and love interest is one of the few people in the neighborhood who does not fear him. In fact she stands up to him and has rejected him on several occasions. Nour is in love with Sherief, a deputy public prosecutor whose personal beliefs and work ethics are against everything that Hatem stands for. Envious of Nour and Sherief's relationship, Hatem assaults, abuses and rapes Nour in an attempt to keep her to himself. Nour comes home with blood on her clothes, shaken, scared and in tears. A doctor confirms that Nour was assaulted and raped, which fuels her mother to hit the streets and begin a riot supported by people of the area. The whole neighborhood gathers in a protest to prosecute Hatem. Hatem is eventually killed during the riot. The film highlights a very important and relevant issue in Egypt – police brutality and injustice. This film predicted a nation-wide revolution, years prior to the Egyptian uprising in 2011.

Hassan wa Morcos (Hassan and Marcus)

The lives of a Muslim Sheikh and a Christian priest are endangered by religious extremists in this pre-revolution film released in 2008. For their safety and well-being, the Egyptian government places the two men and their families in a witness protection program that requires them to disguise themselves. The Muslim Sheikh Mahmoud is disguised as a Christian man assuming the name Morcos Abdel-Shahid, while the Christian priest Boulos, disguises himself as a Muslim Sheikh named Hassan. The two families end up living in the same building and form a close friendship. They survive difficulties of prejudice and social harassment, which causes sectarian violence.

The women in this film are portrayed as religious and devoted to their families. Each stands by her husband's side in any decision that he takes. The two wives and the Sheikh's daughter all follow the patriarchal system, but are not submissive enough to remain silent. The film depicts a lot of flaws in the political sphere, starting with the fact that when Hassan joins the witness protection program, he changes his identity from a Christian to a Muslim. He was also accused of being a radical Islamist though there was no evidence against him. Additionally, when problems occur between the Muslims and the Christians in the small community where Hassan and Morcos live, the two families gather together to rally for peace between the Muslim and Christian Egyptians, since the government failed to do so themselves.

Welad el Amm (*Escaping Tel Aviv*)

Welad el Amm known in English as *Escaping Tel Aviv* was released in 2009. After going on a boat trip with her husband of seven years and two kids, Salwa finds herself surrounded by Israeli forces as her husband confesses to her that he is an Israeli Intelligence officer. He kidnaps the family and forces them to flee to Israel. Egyptian intelligence officer Moustafa gets assigned to rescue Salwa and her kids and bring them back to Egypt safely. Salwa has the weight of the world on her shoulders as she is forced to fight for her children and her country, whilst trying to escape from her husband and from Israel.

Salwa is an elegant woman, who is reluctant to work with the Egyptian Intelligence to bring down her husband and betray him despite his deception. She cares deeply for her family and has immense faith in her religion, Islam. She is portrayed as a courageous and strong woman who is forced to be mentally, emotionally and physically strong, as the fate of her family depends on her.

Ehky ya Shahrazad (*Shahrazad, Tell Me a Story*)

In this 2009 pre-revolution film, Heba is an opinionated and strong woman, who works as a talk show host, drawing attention to controversial issues and issues related to women. Her husband works for a newspaper company that supports the government and is awaiting a promotion. After learning about his wife's views, his superiors at the newspaper ask him to control his wife and what she reports in her show or risk his promotion. Heba's husband tries to seduce her and uses several tactics to subtly change her mind about the topics that she reports. He succeeds in manipulating her for some time. However, Heba once again returns to the controversial topics that are important to her and her viewers. Heba features women who are part of some of Egypt's biggest social problems on her show, which consequently points a finger at the government. She gets physically abused by her husband for promoting such information and goes on to report the abuse on national television. Heba's show is a threat to the government's political agenda, as she highlights some of the worst kinds of social issues in the country. Although she is asked to stop, Heba continues to highlight problems in Egyptian society and questions the authoritative system. Heba is interviewed with her face covered in bruises and she exposes the government and the manipulative ways they use to silence her and the stories of the impoverished communities. The film attempts to tackle important issues about social injustice, abuse, harassment, violence and the most significant topic – justice for women.

Cairo 678

The 2010 film focuses on the lives of three separate women, Fayza, Seba and Nelly. Fayza is from a low-income family and lives a very simple life, she experiences sexual harassment on a daily basis on her commute to and from work as she takes the public bus. The emotional scarring from sexual harassment has left her without any sexual desires towards her husband.

Seba is a jewelry designer from a middle-income family. She is sexually assaulted by a gang of men while in a stadium with her husband. Her husband suddenly leaves her, unable to make sense of what has happened, and she is physically and emotionally abandoned. Seba then starts a support group for victims of harassment.

Nelly portrays a comedian and a customer service representative, who is regularly harassed on the phone. On her way home, she gets roughed up by a truck driver, who was attempting to sexually abuse her. She holds onto the truck until people arrive to help her, but when she goes to the police, they tell her that if they file a police report she will be humiliated all over the country for allowing someone to harass her. She then takes matters into her own hands and reports her story on television.

The girls, particularly Nelly and Seba, challenge authority as they go public with their concerns over women's rights and the harassment that women receive on a daily basis on the streets of Cairo. During her comedy show, which has a large audience base, Nelly confronts the issue of harassment by sharing her story and the police's reaction to her report against her harasser. Eventually, Nelly goes on national television to report harassment to the whole of Egypt, after the police officer at the station advised her not to go public with her complaint and refused to file a report for her.

Bentein Men Masr (*Two Girls from Egypt*)

This 2010 film features Hannan and her cousin Dalia, two unmarried women in their early thirties. Given that Egyptian women usually get married in the early to mid-twenties, Hannan and Dalia are on a mission to find a man, any man. Their need to get married becomes so pressing that they lower their standards, and even humiliate themselves. Hannan, for example, is so determined to get married that she agrees to taking a virginity test, to prove to her suitor that her hymen has not been touched hoping to appease her male companion. After this he abandons her because he was not ready to be in a relationship. The idea of being unmarried is so daunting that Hannan even asks to borrow her friend's baby in an attempt to experience the joy of breast feeding. The scene is disturbing and powerful, as it portrays the wrong perception which Egyptian women nurture often assuming that their only capability is to become a wife. This is although Hannan is employed in a good position in a library and has received praise for her work. The film is controversial as it highlights some of the social issues that have kept the country shackled. Throughout the film, one can see images of protests and revolutions, while many foster a desire to flee the country illegally.

The film addresses the traditional misogynistic stereotypes about women, and their roles in society.

Asmaa

Asmaa a controversial film that was released in 2011, is based on a true story about a poor woman who has been diagnosed with AIDS, a huge taboo in Egypt. Asmaa is a widow, who contracted AIDS from her husband and is now living with her father and daughter. Afraid of the social ostracisation, Asmaa struggles to live in a society which has forced her to keep her illness a secret. One opportune day she is offered a chance to appear on a television talk show, after doctors refused to operate on her erupting gallbladder because she confessed to having AIDS. Sadly, the film is based on a true story. The talk show is intended to bring awareness about the misconceptions of AIDS and the social stigma in Egypt that is discriminating to people like Asmaa. It also tackles the serious lapses in medical treatment in Egypt, while addressing the way in which the poor are unfairly treated, and how the government's injustice has harmed the underprivileged.

Humiliated because of her disease, Asmaa has been so secretive about her condition that her daughter does not know that she is sick. When given the opportunity to go public with her disease on a national television show that discusses social problems in Egypt, Asmaa reluctantly agrees to go live with her story. She discusses her illness, struggles and obstacles, and the medical system that failed her, after they abandoned her mid-surgery, when they discovered that she has AIDS. The television show host, blames the political system that has created a gap between the societal classes. Thus, people like Asmaa, who come from lower-income families are mistreated by the government and society.

Fatat al Masna (*Factory Girls*)

The 2013 film features girls who come from impoverished homes and work in a textile factory. As one girl is infatuated with the supervisor of the factory that she works in, an out of wedlock pregnancy ensues (this is shameful and punishable in Egypt, particularly amongst the poor and uneducated). The film depicts the lives of the factory workers and their societal class and their daily struggles.

This film features Hayam who is part of the lower rungs of the economic class of Egypt. Therefore, her hair is always covered and she is dressed in conservative clothing. Hayam follows the family rules and takes responsibility for the household chores. However, this makes her feel empty and she is often seen gossiping about boys or staring at the factory manager Salah. Although she follows the family rules she still attempts to talk and flirt with men to find contentment. The film shows Hayam as one who, although insecure and fragile, is still strong enough to support herself and to find ways to change her fate, despite the price she may have to pay.

The women characters in the pre and post revolution films are also fighters like their counterparts of the Golden Era, and their struggles are both for social and personal causes. Their suffering gives them the impetus to fight discrimination by society and the government including malpractices in the medical and police system. Current problems like public harassment and domestic violence are addressed by the heroines and the focus is on reforming the social and governmental structure. The use of media to publicise traumatic events and garner support to fight it, is typical of this period. This is in keeping with the general estimation of the Arab Spring as a social media revolution.

CHAPTER 5

Changing Roles: A Comparison of the Two Eras

Women have always played significant roles in the Egyptian film industry. Inspirational singers like Umm Kalthoum, Laila Mourad, Fairouz, Shadia and other prominent figures helped shape the industry, while representing the Egyptian women of the time. Actresses such as Hend Rostom, Faten Hamama and Madiha Yousry used their talent to defy cultural norms and fight for women's rights in front of the camera. Women make up 49.4% of Egypt's population (The World Bank 2017) and so are a 'bright absentee' in its socio-political narrative. It is important also to note the powerful impact that cinema has on a society, particularly one like Egypt, where the industry has a massive economic footprint and is the largest in the region. Thus, it is vital that Egyptian women are celebrated in such an industry that is used as a force of influence and power not just in Egypt but in the wider Arab world as well.

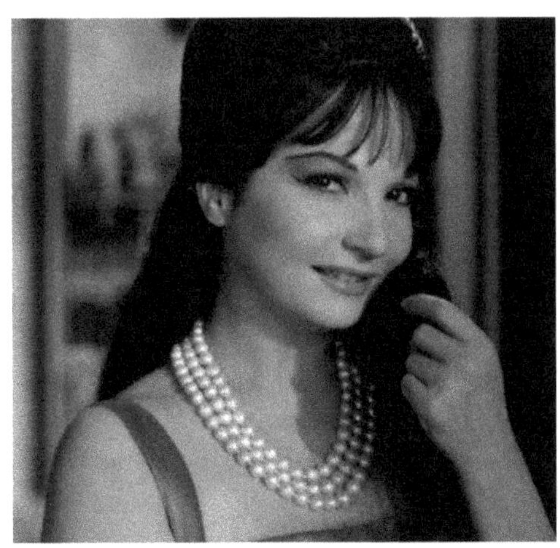

Shadia, Egyptian actress and singer popular during the Golden Age and beyond

The study of the portrayal of women in the Golden Age era and the pre/post Revolution era of Egyptian cinema was conducted to understand the role of women in Egyptian society and the evolution from what is believed to be the oppressive, patriarchal system of the 1940s to the 1960s, to the pre/post revolution heroines. Although women of the Golden Age followed a strict patriarchal system, it did not mean that they were not fighting for their liberation. In fact, it is evident throughout this study that they have taken to the streets and rallied for political freedom and to gain personal rights such as the right to work and get an education. Most importantly they were able to force a redraft of the constitution. Today, Egyptian women have the right to education and to follow a career and the government has taken affirmative action to see a larger female presence in the parliament.

However, Egyptian women have a new struggle to champion which is against social injustices such as rigid dress codes, harassment, discrimination and more. Analysis of Golden Age and pre/post revolution Egyptian cinema throws light on the progress in women's emancipation from one decade to another, emphasizing that the rights of women were earned through continuous struggle against the authoritarian political regime. In both periods the women characters were fighting for their rights but what changed is the milieu. Interestingly in the second cohort many heroines have media-related jobs. This was the period when after the fall of Mubarak, Egyptian media blossomed suddenly emboldened by the freedom from political repression.

In the Golden Age, women were fighting for the freedom to work and gain an education. In the 1970s and 1980s, women joined men in their fight to maintain Egypt as an independent state against Israel. In the 2000s, Egyptian women continue to fight for their personal freedom and gender equality. Though there is positive change in women's status new issues surface and the struggle continues. Today, Egyptian women are a prominent corrective force in society, tackling controversial issues that would otherwise be swept under the carpet. Important issues such as marital abuse, AIDS, corruption, poverty and illiteracy are made the subject of films too. Films portray women in the lead, defying the odds and challenging authority within the public sphere, unafraid of the consequences. Art represents life and interestingly the films chosen demonstrate how female empowerment has been achieved over the decades and the role the cinema industry played to facilitate gender equality. It also showcases the strength that women have to challenge authority.

Although the persona of the women of the Golden Age and the pre/post-revolution era are similar, there are significant differences in how the women are portrayed on screen. To begin, in the Golden Age of Egyptian Cinema, women who smoked and drank alcohol were considered posh and attractive. In the pre/post-revolution era, smoking and drinking is considered inappropriate and vulgar. In films from both eras educated women wore Western clothing, though in the cinema of the Golden Age women rarely covered their hair, unless they came from the countryside or farming community. In both eras, women who are members of impoverished communities are often found dressed conservatively with their hair covered, and following a patriarchal system in which their father or husband is the dominant force in their lives. The number of women characters who were shown consuming alcohol also dwindled in the chosen films of the pre/post revolution era. However, irrespective of their societal class, it was evident that the women from different communities across Egypt were not afraid to speak up or protest against injustice. As seen, several films that were analysed saw everyday women protesting against the system and actively being involved within the society.

Political themes are rare in the Golden Age but are ubiquitous in the pre and post revolution films. Women characters in the latter cohort are vocal about their political opinions. In the Golden Age film *Al Bab Al Maftouh*, however, the protagonist is a female who plays a prominent role by encouraging her brother and cousin to travel to the Egyptian city of Port Said to fight against Israel. She is also seen as a passionate activist who leads many political rallies in her school, asking for the male students to join the fight. This film is a rare glimpse of political activism, particularly from a female character. There are few films from the Golden Age of Egyptian Cinema that challenge the regime or the system.

The pre-/post-revolution films however, continuously challenge the government. In films like *Heya Fawda*, the plot is based on police brutality, which results in a revolution against the police and the government. This film was aired in 2007, four years prior to the uprising. Other films from the pre-/post-revolution era, attempt to tackle social issues, pointing a finger at the government. Most of the films that challenge the government have strong female characters that are not afraid to publicly voice their opinions and express their frustration, lead protests and put up a fight in order to alter the system. Many of the films draw on satire as a means to criticise the government.

Private and public spheres

The Golden Age era focused more on women's private sphere while the revolution era films show them in the public arena. German sociologist and philosopher Jürgen Habermas (1989; p. 123), identified 'public sphere', as a social community, which may not have a defined physical space, but in which people can come together to discuss ideas and societal concerns. This seems to define the social dialogues that led to and followed the Revolution. In the case of the 2011 Egyptian uprising, the public sphere takes the form of the internet, where Facebook and Twitter gathered men and women from all walks of life to unite under one common purpose. Habermas identifies the public sphere as a form of communication that is made up of a gathering of private people, expressing the needs of the public within society (1989; p. 124). In the film *Ehky ya Shahrazad* (*Shahrazad, Tell Me a Story*), the public sphere is a television studio, in which women facing serious social issues come forth to present their stories on national television. By using this media platform, the women are publically pleading for their lives and justice. The television host, Shahrazad, rightfully accuses the government of betraying the women on her show. By sharing their stories and decisions on national television, the show gives an opportunity for women across the country to have an opinion on such social issues that may have been too controversial to discuss publicly. The public sphere is therefore a space that encourages opinions, information and decisions to serve a change in society that has 'legitimate authority in any functioning democracy' (Rutherford 2000; p. 18). Other films that use the public sphere to voice their objections are *Cairo 678*, where women confront the very serious issue of public harassment in Egypt, and *Asmaa*, where the protagonist, Asmaa, uses television as a platform to discuss her life after being diagnosed with AIDS. The film also highlights the plight of health care, focusing on the irresponsibility of hospitals and lack of skills of doctors suggesting that governmental corruption has caused degeneration in the health care system in Egypt.

It is believed that the effectiveness of the public sphere depends on the participation of the society and social organizations who act as mediators of social change. In the film, *Heya Fawda* (*This Is Chaos*), Nour and her family use the streets of Shobra in Cairo – the public sphere – in order to fight government corruption and police brutality. Public protests against the police over the issue of rape saw hundreds participating, eventually bringing down the leaders of the corrupt police force. This 2007 film highlighted the twin causes of the nationwide revolution – government corruption and police brutality.

In real life political drama, during the uprising in Egypt, former presidents Hosni Mubarak and Mohamed Morsi were ousted, upon the demand of the nation. It was proven that even women, who were often dismissed by the male-dominated society as ineffective, could bring about social change. In the 2011 revolution, Egyptian women gained massive popularity as they appeared in the public sphere. 'Women have been able to assert themselves in the public sphere through their religion, class, sexuality, family, fashion and other cultural belongings' (Haghani 2015; p.164). In 2014, the Egyptian Constitution added a new regulation that would take 'the necessary measures to ensure appropriate representation of women in legislative bodies and high public posts' (Center of Arab Woman for Training and Research 2014; p.51). Not only were women recognized as members of parliament, but certain laws, regulations and governmental efforts were put in place to protect the rights and well-being of Egyptian women. One of the primary concerns of female Egyptian nationals is the issue of street harassment and both men and women joined a public movement demanding the safety for women on the streets of Egypt. According to a United Nations study, 'nine out of ten Egyptian women have experienced some form of sexual assault, ranging from minor harassment to rape', making this issue a top priority for women and subsequently, for the government. Sure enough, in 2014 a new law was formed in Egypt that would protect women from harassers. Law breakers would face anywhere from six months to five years in prison, depending on the extent of their crime (BBC 2014). Interestingly enough, in the film *Heya Fawda* the protest against police brutality, assault, rape and harassment, is led by three women, who together manage to organize a rally.

Incremental reforms

Egypt became a constitutional monarchy in 1923, when King Fouad took over the country and appointed as Prime Minister, Saad Zaghloul whose *Wafd* party won with an overwhelming majority. During this time, the middle class Egyptian began to espouse education and the number of government schools for girls continued to rise, thus creating more female graduates (Haghani 2015; p. 165). With the tradition of veiling and seclusion in decline, women were permitted to attend university and have a visible presence in the public sphere. The women's movement continued to expand a decade later, as journals published by women increased the awareness of the female presence. This is when women started to make a mark in the public sphere, appearing in public entertainment such as concerts, art exhibitions, films, musical and theatrical performances and many more. Education thus transformed the country from a state that was repressive towards women, to a state that allowed the participation of men and women across the social spectrum. This contributed to the proliferation of a visible national culture shared by both genders and different social classes (Haghani 2015, p. 165). The transformation from traditional gender roles of housewives to women empowered through education and ambition is evident in several films from the Golden Age of Egyptian Cinema including *Ana Horra* (*I Am Free*), in which Amina, breaks the patriarchal system in her house, that demands she gets married and takes care of her family. Amina breaks the family norm and attends university, in order to have a good job that will provide a livelihood. It is only after she gets her Bachelor's Degree, becomes employed, and is living independently, that she decides to get married. This pattern is seen in other films such as *Banat Hawa* (*Daughters of Eve*), in which Esmaat has ambitions that she will one day work in the parliament (a dream that is not achieved), and *Al Ostaza Fatma* (*Ms. Fatma*), in which Fatma enrolls in a university in order to become a lawyer despite her fiancé telling her that she is not fit to be a lawyer because 'it's a man's job'. Fatma is so determined to become a lawyer that her education and her work become a priority over her love interest. During a scene, where she argues with her fiancé Adel over her job, Adel asks her to close her practice and stay at home to serve him as his wife, as the job of a lawyer is too manly for a woman. Fatma replies:

> 'Am I missing an arm? Missing a leg? No tongue? From this day forth I will prove to you that a woman can be better than any man. I know why you men want to bring us down, and not allow us to work, so we can be under your control, to dress you and become servants under your feet. This was in the olden days, the days of our grandparents, the days of the stone-age, but now we have freedom and this country needs both men and women. I mean, women and men.'

Habermas (1991; p. 6) defines a nation as an imagined political community. The community is imagined because members of even the smallest nation will never meet most of its members. Yet in outlook and ideas all the members of the nation remain the same, despite not knowing one another. Thus in their minds, they have a uniform though imagined idea of what their community should adhere to. As stated in the above films, once this imagined idea is under attack, community members will rebel, in order to change the system, so that the nation can correspond with their imagined ideas.

The film *Bentein Men Masr* (*Two Girls from Egypt*) portrays the cultural norm of Egypt in which women must be married by their early twenties. This norm stalls Egyptian society's progress as it prioritizes marriage and family above work and education. In *Bentein Men Masr* both Hannan and Dalia are yearning to marry. Love does not matter to the girls, their only concern is marriage. Both the women have passed the traditional marriage age and are in their late twenties to early thirties. Although one is a doctor and the other has a reputable job, their lives are not satisfying as they are unwed. With society's emphasis on marriage, the women are convinced that the only way that they can be happy and successful in life is through marriage. Thus, their search for a spouse and the extent of their desperation increases throughout the film. The theory of imagined community is at play here. What is imagined is that marriage and family are the only possible routes to a successful and content life. This is an ongoing trend in Egyptian cinema as the portrayal of women in many films emphasize the importance of being married and raising a family. This is also a true reflection of Egyptian society, as marriage and bearing children have become a major priority for many families. According to the Arab Development Report (2004), women who deviate from the norms are often portrayed as malicious and immoral beings whose primary goal in life is to seek pleasure and an extra-marital relationship. 'All she wants is to catch a man, any man, since this is every woman's highest goal' (Ramzi, cited in Arab Development Report 2004; p. 157).

Religion defining women's roles

A study of Arab femininity shows that 'being a woman' is an expectation of women in the Arab world. In the 1980s and 1990s, the Arab world saw a deluge of publications, conferences and seminars that examined women's rights and gender relation issues in Islam. Taking into consideration Islam's influence in gender practices in the Arab world and the West's view of the stereotypically oppressed Muslim woman, a number of feminist scholars felt the need for studies that re-evaluate the gender relations and status of women in Islam (Sabry 2011; p. 165).

Many scholars have evaluated gender discourses in the Islamic context as a series of patriarchal values, while others have suggested that socio-cultural Islamic views towards gender are reassuring and vouch that women have security and dignity (Moghissi 1999; p. 74). Though many scholars believe in the patriarchal traditions of Islam, some scholars have argued from a different perspective. They contend that the Islamic traditions suggest that women should live an unrestricted life that 'true' Islam represents (Sabry 2011; p. 165). In the film *Al Anessa Hanafi* (*Miss Hanafi*), Hanafi is a misogynistic and oppressive man with dictator-like personality traits. Living with his father, step mother and step sister, Hanafi feels the need to torment his step-sister by locking windows tightly so that she does not see the outside world, claiming that it is sinful and disrespectful. Additionally, he comments on her choice of clothing, arguing that her dresses and skirts are too revealing and sinful and immoral. It is not until a minor surgery takes a turn for the worst when Hanafi has an accidental sex change that he begins to understand the problems that women face in a male-oriented family.

The issue of institutionalized sexism has fuelled heated discussions between secular and Muslim Arab feminists about the influence of religion on women's status in Islam (Kabesh 2003). Secular Arab feminists strongly believe that gender oppression and inequality is a result of religious teachings (El Saadawi 1997; p. 135). However, Muslim feminists believe that religion liberated Muslim women and gave them more rights (Ahmed 1992). In her book, *The Veil and the Male Elite*, feminist scholar, Fatima Mernissi (1992, as cited in Sabry 2012; p. 165) argues that the Quran has been interpreted and arranged to submit women to male interests. Her exposition of Islamic feminism suggests that due to false interpretations, the message of Islam has been ignored and reworded to fit an unethical and repressive tradition. Mernissi also examines the Prophet Mohammed's Hadiths (a text that reports of the Prophet's actions, words, messages and habits) and argues that the interpretations contradict the message of Prophet Mohammad. Mernissi believes that the message was meant to break misogynist, pre-Islamic traditions. She adds that throughout history, the patriarchists used the 'isnad' (the series of testimonies which a hadith would be attested by) to understand the Prophet's message, in a manner which served the sexual and political interest of the male elite. Mernissi points out that the dictate to wear the hijab and the isolation of sexes considered an obligatory part of Islam is a fabrication that was put together during the colonial period by male Arab nationalists, and is practiced today by many Islamist groups, as 'a way to secure their dominion in the face of change' (Mernissi 1992, as cited in Sabry 2012; p. 165). In the film *Meraty Modeer Aam* (*My Wife the General Manager*), Esmat has been promoted to a new office as the general manager of the division. Shocked to find out that their new leader is a woman, the men in the office are disgruntled and unsure of how to report to their new superior. Abdel Hadi, the most religious and oldest member of the office believes that Esmat is not fit for the position, because of her gender. A female leader is also unacceptable to Abdel Hadi, who must regularly perform *'wudu'* (Islamic cleansing ritual), every time they shake hands or have any form of physical contact. Thus Abdel Hadi has his bath slippers at hand so that he keeps himself cleansed at all times – insinuating that women may not be pure. This film is a comedy, and pokes fun of the overt and extreme religious behavior.

A three-stage model of responding to oppressive conditions

Author Alfred Alschuler (1986) suggests that individuals go through three stages in their life, in order to gain empowerment and defeat oppression. The first is the 'magic conforming stage' in which individuals are not aware that they are being oppressed and act in compliant ways. The second stage is known as the 'reforming stage' where an individual becomes distressed with those who break the law. The final stage is known as the 'critical transforming stage', where the individuals are made aware that they are being oppressed by an unjust system, so they come together to change their situation. Alschuler (1986) also suggested that as individuals pass through each stage, they become enlightened and become more confident and proactive. This staggered transformation can be witnessed in women characters portrayed in Egyptian cinema. In the film *Welad el Amm* (*Escaping Tel Aviv*), Salwa and her children are kidnapped by her husband, who confesses to her that he is an Israeli spy living in Egypt, and goes by the name of Daniel. Shocked, Salwa starts searching for an Arab national in Israel hoping he will help her get home. Unable to find a solution, Salwa begins to accept her new life in Israel and starts to trust her husband Daniel again, though she is fearful of him. Salwa eventually meets Mostafa, an Egyptian national who works for the Egyptian Intelligence Agency and has been assigned to bring Salwa and her children back to their home. This is when Alschuler's stage transformations are seen at play. When Mostafa explains the danger that Salwa and her children are in, Salwa does not agree and believes that her husband is a good man. This is Alschuler's magic conforming stage, in which Salwa is not aware of the extent of danger that her husband has put her through, and the oppressive lifestyle that he has enforced on her. Secondly, Salwa becomes uneasy when asked to violate her husband's privacy. For instance she is asked to access her husband's personal documents and take their photos. Salwa feels this is invasive and unlawful, which is a description of Alschuler's second stage of transformation, the reforming stage. Finally, Salwa begins to realize that she has been oppressed, and is constantly in fear of her husband who has threatened to kidnap the children if she does not abide by his rules. She decides to do as Mostafa tells her and escapes with her children to go back to Egypt and live her life freely. Daniel finds a way to follow Salwa and tries to kill her. However, Mostafa gets in the way and kills Daniel before he kills his wife. Though her husband and the father of her children is dead, Salwa is not despondent. She is optimistic knowing that she and her family are finally safe. She reaches the final step of Alschuler's stage theory, the critical transformation stage.

Institutionalized sexism

According to authors Feagin and Feagin (1978), Egyptian women regularly experience institutionalized sexism, which is defined as behaviours or mannerisms carried out by males to show their authority over females.

Feminists Collin MacCabe and Laura Mulvey (1989) argued that the female sexuality is the only way in which women can make themselves visible in a male-dominated world. Additionally, institutional sexism (which is prevalent throughout the studied films) can be interpreted as a system of unearned advantages, which allow men complete domination over women (McIntosh 1998). Therefore, institutional sexism prevents women from enjoying equal opportunities and egalitarianism, thus creating a barrier that prevents personal growth and self-fulfillment (Archer et al. 2006). Such is the example with the 1964 film *Lel Regal Fakat* (*For Men Only*), when protagonists Salwa and Elham are not given a chance to complete their engineering project as they are required to work in the desert, which is deemed a man's job. Elham, furious about her manager undermining her intellect and abilities simply because she is a woman, says, 'The manager says we cannot do a man's job. How does he know? Has he even given us a chance? Women can do anything men can do and more! Elham convinces Salwa to join her as they embark on a mission to the desert to meet with their male colleagues to complete the project. They disguise themselves as men and head to the desert, where they manage to fool all their co-workers into thinking that they too are men. It is not until after the project is successfully completed that the true identities of Elham and Salwa are discovered. This is an example of how Egyptian women are deprived of fulfilling careers and prestigious positions. In fact, it was not until 2007 that women finally began to appear as judges in criminal cases (International Herald Tribune 2007).

Egyptian women have kept an ongoing fight against institutional sexism and they are becoming more successful in their fight. Aside from their own struggles, Egyptian women have required governmental aid to enhance the position of women. Arab women's movements such as the Arab Women Speak Out project started by Johns Hopkins University Center for Communication Programs in 1999 inspired Egyptian women to further discuss their circumstances and improve their self-image and take action to change the way in which women are perceived in Egyptian society (Jabre et al 1997; p. 1).

Conclusion

Gender inequality is an on-going issue across the globe and affects millions of women. An effective approach to making a quick transformation in society is by actively endorsing change. This requires a prominent platform that features reputable figures who can support this change, ensuring the ideas of a society's transformation can reach a larger audience. Such was the case with the Golden Age era in which many actresses and directors were at the forefront fighting for the liberation of women against the strict patriarchal system and the right to education for women. Films that confront these (then) controversial issues and feature strong and prominent actresses who portray the roles of the ambitious women subjected to the limiting stern patriarchal system are iconoclastic and visualize the breaking of cultural taboos.

This study concludes that women of the 1940s to 1960s did not necessarily abide by the patriarchal system or allow oppression to take control of their actions and their lives. In fact, it was this very system that helped them become stronger to face adversity. The films analysed from the period also express the same sentiment. Similarly, this was the case for the Revolution in 2011, in which women fought against oppression and inequality on the streets of Cairo. Cinema and media in general played a vital role in this era, particularly post revolution. Films produced highlighted some of the biggest concerns of Egyptian women and even recreated the most inspirational women's stories as biopics. Films of the period featured several realities of the revolution including scenes of women actively protesting and leading public rallies. The story line of some of the films featured talk show hosts and chat shows that discussed political events and included females. This faithfully represented the new Egypt after the fall of Mubarak were media received a shot of freedom and evolved into a mature platform to promulgate democracy and depict women playing a significant role in society.

Even when society at large was patriarchal and oppressed women the selected heroines displayed determination just like many real life iconoclasts. As seen in this study, films have recorded the unfolding of history and at times been a forerunner, setting the scene for events to unfold. Art imitates life and life imitates art in a relentless cycle enriching our socio-cultural experiences.

Bibliography

Abdel Raouf, A. (2004). *The Social Status of the Egyptian Woman as Presented on the Egyptian Television and its Relevance to Real Life: An Applied Analytical Study*. Unpublished PhD Dissertation. Cairo University – Mass Communication Studies.

Abou Shadi, A. (1998). *Ittijāhāt al-sīnimā al-Miṣrīyah*. al-Qāhirah: Dār al-Aḥmadī lil-Nashr.

Afshar, H. (1996). Women and Politics of Fundamentalism in Iran. In: H. Afshar, ed., *Women and Politics in the Third World*, 1st ed. London: Routledge.

Agwa, A. (2000). The image of Women Portrayed in the Egyptian Movies Broadcast on Channel One on the Egyptian TV. *Cairo University*.

Ahmed, L. (1992). *Women and gender in Islam*. New Haven CT: Yale University Press

Ali, S. (2013). Race: The Difference That Makes a Difference. *CC Creative Commons*, 11(1).

Alschuler, A. (1986). Creating a World Where It Is Easier To Love: Counseling Applications of Paulo Freire's Theory. *Journal of Counseling & Development*, 64(8), pp.492-496.

Amin, G. (2000). *Whatever happened to the Egyptians?*. Cairo: American University in Cairo Press.

Anderson, B. (1991). *Imagined communities*. New York: Verso.

Archer, L., Riley, S. and Veseley, L. (2006). *Institutional Sexism in Academia*. [online] University of Leicester. Available at: http://www.le.ac.uk/pc/jrb/Approach/Riley2006.pdf [Accessed 2 Dec. 2015].

Armes, R. (1987). *Third World film making and the West*. Berkeley: University of California Press.

Armes, R. (2015). *New voices in Arab cinema*, Bloomington: Indiana University Press.

Asante, M. (2002). *Culture and customs of Egypt*. Westport, Conn.: Greenwood Press.

Ateya, A. (2014). Women Empowerment as Portrayed Through The Egyptian Cinema: Content Analysis of Films Produced Between 2001-2011. *American University in Cairo*, [online] 10(1). Available at: http://jmem.gsu.edu/files/2014/10/JMEM-2014-ENG-Aya.pdf [Accessed 8 Dec. 2015].

Awad, S. and Wagoner, B. (2018). *Street art of resistance*. Cham: Palgrave MacMillan, pp.4-8.

Bandhauer, A. and Royer, M. (2015). *Stars in world cinema: Screen Icons and Star Systems Across Cultures*. London: I.B Tauris.

Baron, B. (1994). The women's awakening in Egypt: culture, society, and the press. *Choice Reviews Online*, 32(03), pp.32-1708-32-1708.

BBC News. (2014). Egypt brings in new sex assault laws. [online] Available at: https://www.bbc.com/news/world-middle-east-27726849 [Accessed 5 May 2016].

Boraïe, S., Darwish, M., Ṣabbān, R. and Alwan, Y. (2008). *The golden years of Egyptian film*. Cairo: The American University in Cairo Press.

Botman, S. (1988). *The rise of Egyptian communism, 1939-1970*. Syracuse, N.Y.: Syracuse University Press.

Center of Arab Woman for Training and Research,. (2014). *Women in Public Life – Gender, Law and Policy in the Middle East and North Africa* (P. 51). Paris: OECD Publishing.

Central Agency for Public Mobilization and Statistics (1972). *Al-Mar'at al-Masritya fi ishrin Am 1952-1972*. [online] Cairo: CAPMAS, p.77. Available at: https://www.capmas.gov.eg/ [Accessed 25 Jan. 2019].

Chapple-Sokol, S., Slutzker, J., Middleton-Detzner, A. and Mahmood, S. (2011). Women and the Egyptian Revolution: A Dream Deferred?. *Palestine-Israel Journal of Politics, Economics, and Culture Women and Power*, 17(3-4).

Collette-White, M. (2009). Egyptian film on women's role draws ire and praise. [online] Reuters. Available at: https://www.reuters.com/article/us-venice-egypt/egyptian-film-on-womens-role-draws-ire-and-praise-idUSTRE5832W920090904 [Accessed 27 Dec. 2018].

Creekmur, C. and Mokdad, L. (2012). *The international film musical*. Edinburgh: Edinburgh University Press.

Cornell University Empowerment Group (1989). Empowerment and family support. Networking Bulletin, 1, 1–23.

Dal, M. (2014). *Cairo: Images of Transition*. New York: Columbia University Press, p.250.

Dwyer, K. and Tazi, M. (2004). *Beyond Casablanca*. Bloomington: Indiana University Press.

El Hadidi, M. (1977). Image of Egyptian Women in Egyptian Film and its Social Consequences. Unpublished PhD dissertation, Cairo: Cairo University, Mass Communication Department.

El Saadawi, N. (1997). *The Nawal El Sadaawi reader*. New York: Zed Books.

Enloe, C. (1990). *Bananas, beaches & bases*. Berkeley: University of California Press.

Ewing, E. (2005). *Revolution and pedagogy* (p. 80). New York: Palgrave Macmillan.

Farid, S. (2005). *Surat al-Mar'a fi al-Masrah wal-Sinima (The Image of Women in the Theatre and the Cinema)*. 8th ed. Cairo: Unknown.

Feagin, J. and Feagin, C. (1978). *Discrimination American style*. Englewood Cliffs, N.J.: Prentice-Hall.

Foucault, M. (1970). *The Order of Things*. London: Routledge.

Franco, J. (1994). Beyond Ethnocentrism: Gender, Power and the Third-World Intelligentsia. In: P. Willam and L. Chrisman, ed., *Colonial Discourse and Post-Colonial Theory: A reader*, 1st ed. London: Harvester Wheatsheaf.

Freire, P. (1972). *Pedagogy of the oppressed*. New York: Herder and Herder.

Freire, P. (1976). Education, the practice of freedom. London: Writers and Readers Publishing Cooperative.

Ganti, T. (2012). *Producing Bollywood* (p. 32). Durham: Duke University Press.

Ginsberg, T., & Lippard, C. (2010). *Historical Dictionary of Middle Eastern cinema*. Lanham: Scarecrow Press.

Goldschmidt, A. (2013). *Historical dictionary of Egypt* (p. 40). Metuchen, N.J.: Scarecrow Press Inc.

Habermas, J. (1989). *The Structural Transformation of the Public Sphere*. Cambridge, Mass.: MIT Press.

Hafez, S. (2019). *Women of the Midan: The Untold Stories of Egypt's Revolutionaries*. Bloomington: Indiana University Press, p.85.

Haffner, P. (1997). Water and the Nation. *Ecrans d'Afrique*, 21-22(3rd-4th quarter).

Haghani, F. (2015). Egyptian women, revolution and the making of a visual public sphere. *Journal for Cultural Research*, 19(2), pp.162-175.

Henderson, S. and Jeydel, A. (2007). *Participation and Protest: Women and Politics in a Global World*. New York: Oxford University Press.

Henry, H. (2011). Egyptian women and empowerment: A cultural perspective. *Women's Studies International Forum*, 34(3).

Herrera, L. (2014). *Revolution in the age of social media*. London: Verso, pp.2-5.

Hirsh, E. (1995). Introduction: Landscape: Between Place and Space. In: E. Hirsh and M. O'Hanlon, ed., *The Anthropology of Landscape: Perspectives on Place and Space*, 1st ed. Oxford: Clarendon Press.

International Herald Tribune (2007). Egypt names first women judges. Retrieved April 24, 2007 from. http://www.iht.com/articles/ap/2007/03/14/africa/ME-GEN-Egypt-Women-Judges.php

International Labour Organization (1988). *The Burden of Public Service Employment and Remuneration: A Case Study of Egypt*. Geneva: ILO, p.32.

Jabre, B. Underwood, C. Goodsmith, L. (1997). *Arab women speak out*. Baltimore: Johns Hopkins Center for Communication Programs. Available http://ccp.jhu.edu/documents/Arab%20 Women%20 Speak%20Out-Profiles%20of%20Self-Empowerment. pdf, accessed on 22 February 2019.

Jayawardena, K. (2016). Feminism and nationalism in the Third world. 2nd ed. London: Verso.

Joseph, S. (2000). Gender and citizenship in the Middle East. Syracuse, NY: Syracuse Univ. Press.

Joseph, S. and Najmabadi, A. (2005). Encyclopedia of Women and Islamic Cultures: Family, Law and Politics. Leiden: Koninklijke Brill.

Jumhuriyat Misr (1956). Al Dustur [The Constitution]. Al Matba'a al-Amiria.

Kabesh, A T (2003). Reading the other, women, feminism, and Islam. Studies in Gender and Sexuality, 4, 59–71.

Kamal, H. (2015). Inserting women's rights in the Egyptian constitution: personal reflections. *Journal for Cultural Research*, 19(2), pp.150-161.

Kandiyoti, D. (1994). Identity and its Discontents: Women and the Nation. In: P. William and L. Chrisman, ed., *Colonial Discourse and Post Colonial Theory: A Reader*, 1st ed. London: Harvester Wheatsheaf.

Kaplan, E. (1992). *Motherhood and representation*. London: Routledge.

Keddie, N. (1991). *Women in Middle Eastern History: Shifting Boundaries in Sex and Gender*. New Haven: Yale University Press, pp.310-330.

Keddie, N. and Baron, B. (1991). *Women in Middle Eastern History: Shifting Boundaries in Sex and Gender*. New Haven: Yale University Press, pp.310-330.

Khater, A. (1988). Al-Harakah Al-Nissa'lyah: The women's movement and political participation in modern Egypt. *Women's Studies International Forum*, 11(5).

Khatib, L. (2006). *Filming the modern Middle East*. London: I.B. Tauris.

Khouri, M. (2010). *Arab national project in Youssef Chahine's cinema*. Cairo: American University in Cairo Press.

Kimball, G. (2017). *Brave: Young women's global revolution*. 2nd ed. Chico: Equality Press.

Kurtz, M. and Kurtz, L. (2015). *Women, War, and Violence: Topography, Resistance, and Hope*. 1st ed. Santa Barbara: Praeger, p.335.

Leaman, O. (2001). *Companion encyclopedia of Middle Eastern and North African film*. London: Routledge.

Liggett, H. and Perry, D. (1995). *Spatial practices*. Thousand Oaks, Calif.: Sage Publications.

Lury, K. and Massey, D. (1999). Making Connections. *Screen Autumn*, 40(3).

MacCabe, C. and Mulvey, L. (1989). Images of Women, Images of Sexuality: Some Films by J.L Godard. In: L. Mulvey, ed., *Visual and Other Pleasures: Language, Discourse, Society*, 1st ed. London: Macmillan.

Mariscotti, C. (2008). *Gender and class in the Egyptian women's movement, 1925-1939*. Syracuse, NY: Syracuse University Press.

Mclntosh, P. (1998). White privilege, unpacking the invisible knapsack. In M. McGoldrick (Ed.), Re-visioning family therapy: Race, culture, and gender in clinical practice (pp. 147–152). Guilford Press: New York.

Mechanic, D. (1991). Strategies for Integrating Public Mental Health Services. *Hospital & Community Psychiatry*, 42(8), pp.797-801.

Mekay, E. (2011). *Arab Women Lead the Charge | Inter Press Service*. [online] Ipsnews.net. Available at: http://www.ipsnews.net/2011/02/arab-women-lead-the-charge/ [Accessed 25 Jan. 2019].

Mernissi, F. (1992). *The veil and the male elite*. Reading, Mass.: Addison-Wesley Pub. Co.

Moghissi, H. (1999). *Feminism and Islamic fundamentalism*. London: Zed Books.

Monks, K. (2016). *A new golden age of Egyptian cinema?*. [online] CNN. Available at: https://www.cnn.com/2016/12/06/middleeast/egypt-revolution-cinema/index.html [Accessed 24 Dec. 2018].

Mostafa, D. (2015). Introduction: Egyptian women, revolution, and protest culture. *Journal for Cultural Research*, 19(2).

Naficy, H. (1996). Phobic Spaces and Liminal Panics: Independent Transnational Film Genre. In: W. Dissanayake and R. Wilson, ed., *Global/Local: Cultural Production and the Transnational Imaginary*, 1st ed. London: Duke University Press.

Nelson, C. (1996). *Doria Shafik, Egyptian feminist* (pp. 125-126). Gainesville, Fla.: University Press of Florida.

Nowell-Smith, G. (1996). *The Oxford history of world cinema*. Oxford: Oxford University Press.

Obeidat, R. (2002). *Content and representation of women in the Arab media*. 1st ed. [ebook] Beirut: United Nations – Division for the Advancement of Women (DAW). Available at: http://www.un.org/womenwatch/daw/egm/media2002/reports/EP11Obeidat.PDF [Accessed 5 Dec. 2015].

O'Healy, A. (1999). Revisiting the belly of Naples: the body and the city in the films of Mario Martone. *Screen*, 40(3), pp.239-256.

Pidduck, J. (1998). Of windows and country walks: frames of space and movement in 1990s Austen adaptations. *Screen*, 39(4), pp.381-400.

Ramdani, N. (2013). Women in the 1919 Egyptian Revolution: From Feminist Awakening to Nationalist Political Activism. *Journal of International Women's Studies*, *14*(2), 36-49. Retrieved from http://vc.bridgew.edu/cgi/viewcontent.cgi?article=1679&context=jiws

Ramzi, N. (1995). Comparison between woman's and man's images in Egyptian drama – an analytical study. Cairo: UNICEF.

Rappaport, J. (1987). Terms of empowerment/exemplars of prevention: Toward a theory for community psychology. *Am J Commun Psychol*, 15(2), pp.121-148.

Rappaport, J. (1995). Empowerment meets narrative: Listening to stories and creating settings. *Am J Commun Psychol*, 23(5), pp.795-807.

Rutherford, P. (2000). *Endless propaganda*. Toronto: University of Toronto Press.

Salama, M. (2018). *Islam and the culture of modern Egypt from the monarchy to the republic*. Cambridge: Cambridge University Press, pp.162-163.

Saoub, E. (2011). The unseen factor: Egypt's women protesters | DW | 10.02.2011. [online] DW.COM. Available at: https://www.dw.com/en/the-unseen-factor-egypts-women-protesters/a-14834006 [Accessed 25 Jan. 2019].

Sabry, A. (2011). An Invitation to View the Body of an Egyptian Girl'. *Al-Ahram*.

Sabry, T. (2012). Arab Cultural Studies: Mapping the Field. London: Palgrave Macmillan, p.165.

Shafik, V. (2007). *Arab Cinema: History and Cultural Identity*. Cairo: The American University in Cairo Press.

Shafik, V. (2007). *Popular Egyptian cinema*. Cairo: American University in Cairo Press.

Sorbera, L. (2014). Challenges of thinking feminism and revolution in Egypt between 2011 and 2014. *Postcolonial Studies*, 17(1), pp.63-75.

Sparr, P. (1994). Mortgaging Women's Lives: Feminist Critiques of Structural Adjustment. London: Zed Press, pp.41-43.

Tadros, M. (2016). *Resistance, revolt, and gender justice in Egypt*. Syracuse: Syracuse University Press, p.5-6.

The National. (2009). Mona tells a story. [online] Available at: https://www.thenational.ae/arts-culture/mona-tells-a-story-1.532599 [Accessed 19 May 2019].

United Nations Development Programme, (2005). *Arab Human Development Report 2005*. [online] Available at: http://www.arab-hdr.org/publications/other/ahdr/ahdr2005e.pdf [Accessed 5 Dec. 2015].

Valassopoulos, A. (2013). *Arab cultural studies* (pp. 174-176). London: Routledge.

World Bank,. (2016). *Population, female (% of total) | Data | Table. Data. worldbank.org*. Retrieved 5 May 2016, from http://data.worldbank.org/indicator/SP.POP.TOTL.FE.ZS

Yeganoglu, M. (1998). *Colonial fantasies*. Cambridge, U.K.: Cambridge University Press.

Yousry, J. (2002). College Girls' Perception of their Image as Presented through Arabic Drama. Public Opinion Research Egyptian Magazine, 3 (3). Cairo University, Mass Communication Department, Cairo, Egypt.

Zeitoun, N. (2005). Images of women in contemporary Egyptian film: Elements of the body, sexuality and consumerism (Unpublished master's thesis). Cairo: The American University of Cairo press.

www.ingramcontent.com/pod-product-compliance
Lightning Source LLC
LaVergne TN
LVHW052348100826
845147LV00012B/780

* 9 7 8 1 9 1 2 9 6 9 0 6 7 *